M000202631

NOSTRADAMUS'
DREAM
INTERPRETATION
GUIDE

NOSTRADAMUS'
DREAM
INTERPRETATION
GUIDE

500th Anniversary

1503–2003

Special Edition

by

Dita Arzt-Wegman

2003, Oakville, Canada

Vasitha Publications

Nostradamus

MICHEL NOSTRADAMUS.
Medecin.
Né à St Remy, en Provence, le 14 Decemb. 1503.
Mort le 2 juillet 1566

500th Anniversary

A Tribute to

his life,

his achievements,

and

his legacy.

Nostradamus

1503-2003

- Dita Arzt-Wegman

Nostradamus' Dream Interpretation Guide

All rights (whole or part) reserved, especially concerning translation and
dissemination through public lectures, films, radio, television,
any type of sound carrier, copying, photographic reproduction
or any other form of duplication, or storage by computer.

Copyright © 1998 by Dita (Wegman) Arzt

For more information, contact:
Vasitha Publication,
P.O. Box 70013, 2441 Lakeshore Rd. W., Oakville, ON L6L 6M9 Canada
Fax: (905) 827-8281
E-mail: ditawegman@sympatico.ca
http://www.nostradamusdreams.com

VASITHA

National Library of Canada Cataloguing in Publication

Nostradamus, 1503-1566
Nostradamus' dream interpretation guide / by Dita (Wegman) Arzt
— 500th anniversary 1503-2003 special ed.

Chiefly a translation of Neuestes vollständiges and grösstes
egyptisches Traumbuch, wahrhafte Auslegung aller Träume,
published 1928 ; includes text by the translator, Dita (Wegman) Arzt.
Previously published 1998 under title: Nostradamus' dream book.
ISBN 0-9686022-1-5

1. Dream interpretation. 2. Dreams.
I. Arzt-Wegman, Dietlinde
II. Nostradamus, 1503-1566. Nostradamus' dream book. III. Title.

BF1815.N8N67 2003   135'.3   C2003-900570-4

available in:
English, German, French, Italian & Russian

Design and layout:
Karen Petherick, Intuitive Design International Ltd.
Peterborough, Ontario, Canada
Printed in Canada

TABLE OF CONTENTS

The book known as The Egyptian Dream Interpretation Book, *containing the true interpretations of dreams according to Nostradamus, was last published in Germany in 1928.*

When I was introduced to the volume in 1952, I was fascinated—as I remain today—with the knowledge it contained, and was saddened when I learned that it was no longer in circulation or print, and had even been declared officially lost.

My research in finding the reason why such a rare book could have disappeared is quite astonishing. There was a time period, circa 200 years, reaching as far as into the twentieth century, where writings and documentation associated with the name *Nostradamus* was forbidden in public circulation. Many of the valuables left by him were confiscated and destroyed—lost forever. This desperate action was taken by the reigning monarchs and church authorities who had great political influence. They feared that if the public were to learn an outcome before it was decided—through Nostradamus' accurate prophecies —their dictatorial grip of governing would have been jeopardized.

After World War II, writings by Nostradamus started

to slowly surface again, and his Dream Interpretations were among them.

Thanks to the friend from whom I inherited it, *Nostradamus' Egyptian Dream Interpretation Book* became a joy-giving treasure in my collection, and continued to be, for many decades. Many times has the study of it given me the opportunity to test the accuracy of its method of interpreting the predictive power of dreams. Time and again, I have been amazed by the predictions coming true. It was always a reliable guidance in my life. With great precision and economy of words, Nostradamus focuses on the essential meaning, coming 'right to the point' of the symbols seen in a dream. Elaborate explanations are unnecessary, because what we call a 'dream' is a message in the clear language of symbols as expressed in mental images, reflecting "Nature's Law."

I decided to follow my inspiration and revive this volume so as to preserve for the world Nostradamus' contribution to the understanding of dreams and make it available again to readers everywhere. In this, Nostradamus' 500th Anniversary Edition, the reader will learn the source of prophetic dreams. We can only fathom the mystery of the dream phenomenon by examining more closely its governing power, the activity of the stars and planets: which was also the foundation of Nostradamus' exploration of the universe, a study that he mastered to the highest possible degree, including its influence on our daily lives. Radiations from the eternal world not only connect the planets, stars and our own Earth, but also reach deep into us humans, shaping our sleep and dreams.

By objectively examining the new approach as explained in the following chapters, many will find confirmation of its undeniable substance, while yet others may reject it. I leave it to every individual to decide for him- or herself.

The following chapters are direct translations of the German Edition: *Neuestes vollständiges and grösstes egyptisches Traumbuch, wahrhafte Auslegung aller Träume,* that was last published in 1928.

- Analisation and Meaning of Images Seen in Dreams
- Dreams According to the Zodiac
- Chart of Lucky and Unlucky Days
- Birth month—Characteristics
- Fingernail—Characteristics
- The Art of Laying the Cards
- Dreams Represented in Pictures

In this revised edition, I have included my own writings, as follows:

- Foreword
- Nostradamus—His Achievements, Life and Legacy
- What are Dreams? Fantasies? Or A Message From A Higher Level of Reality
- Exploring the Nature of Sleep. Why Do We Sleep?
- Epilogue
- About the Author

Michael Nostradamus

NOSTRADAMUS—
HIS ACHIEVEMENTS,
LIFE AND LEGACY

When, as a girl in Germany, I first heard the name 'Nostradamus', I experienced what I can only describe as a mystique, a sense of actual mystery with which it seemed to resonate. I felt drawn by that mystery as by a magnet. It was a time when I would gaze, awestruck, at the night stars, and search for the images hidden in their patterns; and in time, I knew the satisfaction of being able to identify them by name, almost as if I had some sort of special connection to them. I would not know the nature of that connection, however, until the day I found myself in the privileged position of rescuing from oblivion the only existing copy of Nostradamus' *Egyptian Dream Interpretation Book*. In the meantime, my admiration for the enigmatic man, who lived 500 years ago, continued to grow.

He is, of course, more popular than ever now for his world prophecies, which are and will be found to be as true as they were when he wrote them. His name is now known in every corner of the earth, and in his own life time he was not only famous, but royalty and other eminent people considered themselves honoured to be his friends.

Why has his fame endured? As is so often the case with extraordinary people, for reasons as variable, and even contradictory, as the reactions they provoke in more run-of-the-mill beings. Many people feel that Nostradamus may well have been the greatest genius who ever lived. Others, perhaps succumbing to the consequences of assuming that if a prediction is fulfilled in a way other than one they would have preferred, the person who made it must be a fraud, see him as a charlatan and mere doomsayer.

Let us delve more deeply to find out who this man really was. Let us pay tribute to his achievements, life and legacy, as we celebrate his 500th anniversary in the year 2003.

Ancestry

Michel de Notredame was born on December 14, 1503 in the diminutive town of St. Remy Provence, France.

His father held the office of notary, and married into the noble house of St. Remy, whose members for generations had maintained close contact with wise emissaries of the Muslim Arab civilization that flourished in neighbouring Spain and was then, in so many ways, so far ahead of Christian Europe. Not only medical and philosophical, but also magical lore suffused that culture, and its currents flowed across and nurtured fertile minds such as those of the St. Remy family.

Archives from that time, document the descent of Nostradamus from a line that is traceable to prophets of the Old Testament. Was this the source of his incredible capacity for seeing the future?

The milieu Michel grew up in was privileged. On his mother's side, his ancestors were known for their skill as physicians; some of them, in fact, were quite famous. The passion of Nostradamus' maternal grandfather, however, was not medicine, but the influence of celestial bodies. It was he who introduced the young future seer to the activity in the Universe through divine power—the driving force behind and within us.

Medicine, nevertheless, took priority in Michel's youthful studies; family tradition, after all, being of great importance then, as it often is now.

Medical Career

Some time around the year 1521 young Michel began his medical studies, in Avignon, France. He had not completed them when the area was devastated by the Black Death (plague); and not only ordinary people, but even his fellow students and the university doctors themselves fled the city.

Michel, however, did not flee. Armed with a courage and what we can only assume to have been extraordinary inner strength, the source of which is bound to remain as mysterious as that of the medical knowledge his actions indicate he possessed, he implemented hygienic and sani-

tary regimes. Needless to say, no one had then heard of
bacteria, viruses or antibiotics; but Nostradamus, whether
acting on sheer inspiration prompted by the genetic legacy
of his mother's family or on information obtained through
his learned Spanish Arab contacts, gave combinations of
herbs to his patients and restored them to health. (The fact
that they were effective against the bubonic plague indicates that the herbs Nostradamus administered must have
had antibiotic properties.) The suffering of many was alle-
viated through his actions, and he not only stopped the
spread of the disease, but eradicated it where it had taken
hold. A tremendous achievement indeed.

The fame that came to Nostradamus at this time
reached the Paris court of King Henry II, and an associa-
tion was formed that, as might be expected, proved of great
consequence in later years.

He was, thus, already a hero among his people when he
passed his medical examination in 1529 at the age of 26.
Shortly thereafter he opened his Medical Practice, married
and fathered two children. In addition to his more spectac-
ular gifts, he was known as a devoted family man, amiable
and good natured; and he possessed, moreover, an excellent
sense of humour.

Astronomy and Astrology

A mind such as Nostradamus' is bound to be restless and constantly questioning, enquiring into matters high and low. He thought about matters most others dared not think about, even had they been capable of doing so; and he would go so far as to seek out the very motivating power of the universe itself. The seeds planted by his grandfather were growing.

Absorbing much of the metaphysical lore concerning correspondences between the high and the low that was pursued in his and nearby cultures, he found what he considered a Universal Law in the precisely repeating patterns revealed by his study of the stars and planets. He devised a mathematical system for calculating the movements of the planets, and used it in his later work of foreseeing earthly events and locating them precisely in time. That is what made him so outstanding from his predecessors in foreseeing the future. The laws governing these matters, he saw as a manifestation of the Power and Wisdom of the Creator.

For him it was essential, that the radiations of the Planets maintain the order and balance of not only human affairs, but the whole of life, as different aspects of the supreme power. They not only support, but influence the existence of all living species—plants and animals and also included, we, as human beings.

Nostradamus' achievements in astronomy and astrology are, perhaps, more than ever recognized today as evidence of a wisdom and inspiration worthy of being called *divine*.

He had great insight into the interwoven nature of the relationship between the material discoveries of man and the laws of the world beyond matter. He understood that the world of matter itself depends on that which is beyond space and time, and is therefore itself a manifestation of Truth.

His approach to philosophical truth about dream interpretation was the same as, and even went beyond that of the wise men of the ancient civilizations of Egypt and

Armillary Sphere: Astronomical Device, 1594-.

Assyria, who studied exclusively celestial bodies, obtaining information and guidance. The same established foundation of knowledge was used, on which the Greeks and Romans continued to build. Documentation for which, can be found in the form of artifacts in the British Museum in London. Nostradamus himself extended that knowledge further through his own research and visionary insight, and bestowed us with his *Egyptian Interpretation Dream Book.*

The Prophet

At the age of 44, in 1547, Nostradamus began making predictions; and from the start, all, including the king, were stunned by his accuracy.

France had been swept a second time by the plague, and those who remembered the role Nostradamus had played the first time, sought his help again, and a second time the doctor-wise man defeated the Black Death. The monarch summoned him to Paris to thank him personally. He was the same king, Henry II, whose death Nostradamus had predicted. Henry's son, Charles IX, made the now extremely famous seer his personal astrologer as well as his personal physician. It was commonplace at the time for a ruling monarch to have frequent recourse to the services of astrologers, and to follow their advice in choosing the timing of important undertakings, including the commencement of efforts to conquer, and through that reliable source, victory was most certain.

In 1555, a year before his death, Nostradamus compiled his collected visions, the results of his nocturnal meditations. He described the process thus:

"When the Light surrounded me and God spoke in the universal language of images, it was not myself, but the divine Light that communicated through me."

Among his most remarkable predictions concerning events in North America were his visions of the assassination of John F. Kennedy, space flight, man's journeying to the moon, and the collapse of communism. It is thought by many that more than half of his prophecies are about events that have yet to occur.

He arranged the visions into almost 1000 Quatrains, and they were later published under the collective title, *Centuries* (the famous *Vierzeiler)*. One of the most famous of them, pointing to our present time, is Quatrain 72 in Century X, often interpreted as referring to August 11, 1999 (using the Gregorian Calendar current in Nostradamus' time).

The content of this prophecy is such that many astronomers and astrologers had asked themselves if it meant the *end of the world*? The tremendous tension generated by the exceedingly rare disposition of the Sun, Moon, Mars, Saturn and Uranus forming a square (solid line) and in addition they faced each other in direct opposite, (interrupted line). It was feared, portended destruction, geological or otherwise, for the human race. The only hope remained in the constellation of Venus-Jupiter (white line).

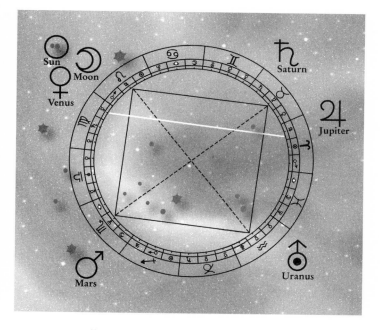

Constellation of the Planets as of August 11, 1999.

As we all know, of course, the world did not end that day: a fact that the sensational media, and some Nostradamus interpreters included, tried to exploit as proof that Nostradamus and his prophecies were and are false. It never occurred to them that they may have misunderstood it, preferring to revel in their own imaginings about its significance.

In order to be able to grasp the real meaning of that date and Nostradamus' prophecy about it, it is necessary to understand that while events on our earthly plane are caused by occurrences that take place on higher levels, the outcome will affect the world of matter, our earth. This is something that takes time to come about, which is a natural process dictated by one of the fundamental laws, namely *cause and effect.*

Was Nostradamus Wrong?

A true prophet is never wrong. *"The messages he is inspired to receive through a Radiant Light are a revelation of the Will of God and are God's Voice as heard by man."* This explanation is from Nostradamus himself.

August 11, 1999 was not (as we know, of course) the end of the world, but rather represented an important turning point for mankind. Some idea of its significance can be arrived at by considering the total eclipse of the sun that occurred on that day, the last one in the just ended century, plunging first the United States into darkness, followed quickly by Europe, and then the Far East. It was a sign for the human race that events of tremendously devastating proportions were imminent. In retrospect we can see it as a warning, especially to world leaders, against (again in Nostradamus' own words) following the wrong path in their decisions, because to do so would have terrible consequences for us all, on this planet.

Visionaries never know the times that their visions will be fulfilled. Had he chosen to do so, Nostradamus could have recorded his visions as he saw them and left it at that. But such was his concern for the generations to follow, that he undertook to find a way in using his mathematical system to identify the times for which each of his warnings was intended, and developed a means of doing so by studying the movement of the planets. It was in this way that he was able to know, and to indicate to us, that August 11, 1999 was the time of which he needed to warn us today. He was the first to do this, to use astrology to locate in time, events foreseen in visions, and he did so using a temporal framework of no less than 500 years.

Another remarkable fact, especially when considering world events then and now, is that something very similar to the unusual arrangement of the planets of which we spoke earlier, also occurred in Nostradamus' own time, which was also turbulent and chaotic, world wide. Verification can be found in the relevant historical works.

What have we, in fact, seen since that date, August 11, 1999? The U.S.A. is at war, and the world itself is walking a dangerous tightrope. The Far East shudders with implicit tensions and the Middle East implodes. Terror spreads— some would say, rules—around the globe. As if human misbehaviour were not enough, natural catastrophes strike hard in all corners. Fires rage, threatening enormous areas in many countries and even some cities. Floods, in a tremendous devastating proportion, stretching from Europe (Italy, Austria, Czech-Republic, Germany to the mid-West in the U.S.A., with deadly mudslides combined, reaching the Far-East and China). Droughts, still continuing in the prairies of Canada, the mid-west United States and Africa, seem to have no end. Volcanoes erupt more frequently and the earth quakes more powerfully than ever before.

"According to Nostradamus, atomic and bio-chemical warfare are imminent, unless our leaders see the wisdom of adopting a gentler approach in solving the conflicts with which our planet rages. Continuing to retaliate with force and to smother the cries of the victims of injustice will, he says, result in World War Three."

At this point we can only say that, once again, he seems to have been on the right track. We will know for sure when it has happened. His sincere wish, however, was not to terrify, but to warn. If our politicians and heads of state act appropriately, putting the concern of human welfare before political gain, destruction can be prevented, and indeed, this is the purpose of prophecy. To enable leaders of nations to see the unavoidable outcome of their actions, and adopt a different course, a more gentler, respectful way, in meeting Nations is one, that will diffuse, not exacerbate, tensions. As has so often in history, if not always, been the case, warnings are dismissed by the majority as nonsense, thus confirming our ignorance and inability to recognize WHO is really in charge, speaking to us through the heavenly bodies, holding both the Universe and our little Earth, with us and our preoccupations on it, in the balance.

Every prophecy comes from God! Its elements consist of knowledge of interconnectedness in the driving force of divine power,

> *and talent for perceiving the past,*
> *the present and the future together*
> *as, manifesting the Will of God.*

Surely the best conclusion to this chapter is to let Nostradamus speak for himself the words from Century III, 94:

> *"For a long time, my knowledge and my work were not fully accepted, nor understood, but rather ignored, but in 500 years from now, in that millennium, a great clarity will come about and through my legacy, mankind's happiness will prevail!"*

Nostradamus' Vision of His Own Death

Shortly before he died, Nostradamus was visited once again by his great admirer and friend of many years, King Charles IX of France. The king came to pay his respects to his long-time personal physician and astrologer, probably not realising it would be the last time they would meet.

The next day, he had spent the evening chatting with another close friend and confidante, de Chavigny. Before his guest left, Nostradamus said to him, "Adieu my friend; tomorrow morning, by sunrise, I will no longer be alive." De Chavigny, needless to say, thought he was joking and didn't pay much attention to his remarks. That following morning, however, Nostradamus, on arising, experienced severe chest pains, sat down on a bench next to his bed, and collapsed. It was July 2, 1556.

Nostradamus had foreseen the circumstances of his death, and recorded them in writing:

There is nothing more to be done. I am going to God!
Next to my bed, on a bench, will they find me—death!

It was exactly thus that he was discovered.

Years later, in a small calendar found in his belongings, next to the date July 2, he had placed a mark and inscribed the Latin words, '*Hic mors prope est*'—'Death is near'. What more compelling verification could there be of the fact that the truth is to be found through a study of the stars?

WHAT ARE DREAMS?—FANTASIES? OR A MESSAGE FROM A HIGHER LEVEL OF REALITY?

*D*reams accompany us on our journey through life, from birth until the end of our time on earth. They originate in the depths of our Soul and reveal themselves to us in pictures without words. We spend almost a third of our life sleeping, entering the subconscious, and yet we pay hardly any attention to this important aspect of our lives. In fact, in our materialistic-oriented and high-tech dominant times, it is almost completely ignored.

Since we now have the knowledge of the origin of Soul/Spirit from the 'Grail Message', a book entitled *In the Light of Truth* (see the Epilogue), we can now separate the two sources of dreams: brain/mind and Soul/Spirit. It is this distinction that is the major key in understanding 'Dreams'. Henceforward I will use the terms 'produced dreams' for those that come from our intellect (or 'big brain'), and 'conceived dreams' for those that come from the subconscious (or 'small brain'). From this profound realization clarity will emerge, and we will be able to correctly categorize and assign the right meaning to what we see in our sleep. We now have the key that will open the door through which we can step into the unknown world beyond, the one that we enter every night in sleep.

Fantasy, or 'Produced Dream'

When we think, our mind is active, or 'producing'. All that we control or initiate, originates in brain activity. For example, we produce thoughts, and indulge in daydreams where 'the sky is the limit'. There is nothing wrong with doing so, if only because life would be dull without building our 'castles in the air' to provide us with some refuge from the sometimes harsh realities of life.

The founder of psychoanalysis, Dr. Sigmund Freud, is well known for his study of dreams that was published some one hundred years ago. However, recent media reports (Neurophantalogue from Austria), have presented his ideas on the subject concerning the definition of Dreams as being less than reliable. His approach tended to see the explanation of dreams in the psychological condition of the individual, and has provided an enormous and fertile territory for psychiatrists and psychotherapists. They have sought to examine the details of the confused pictures, talkings and stories of which dreams consist and that so often leave the dreamer in a state of fear or discomfort creating the so-called 'sleep disorder'. Pursuing this method of dream study requires absorbing the voluminous writings of those who have researched it so far. Unfortunately for those who have adopted Freud's stance, more recent scientific studies have led many to reject his ideas about what he called a 'Dream'. The Sigmund Freud Institute of Germany, after a convention of dream researchers from around the world, published a statement to the effect that dreams are, in fact, nothing more than a *worrisome product of our own thoughts* that we take with us when we fall asleep. In other words, they are only confused stories that we *spit out* after digesting the events of the day. Waking in the morning, often in fear and perspiration is, following this analogy, a kind of *indigestion*.

It is correct to use the term 'analysis' when describing the method of approach to such dreams. It is only by such means that their significance can be discovered.

With a *conceived dream*, on the other hand, it is not analysis, but *intuitive interpretation* that is needed. It is advisable, therefore, to bear in mind that not everything we see in our sleep deserves the name *Dream*.

The Conceived Dream

A dream that is referred to as a *conceived* dream is a different kind of dream from the one we call '*produced*'.

The 'conceiving' process referred to is one that takes place in the subconscious mind, or small brain, during sleep. The small brain is the receiver station, so to speak, and is connected with the waking function of intuition.

The 'producing' process, on the other hand, can only be performed by the conscious mind or intellect, our big brain, that is at work during the waking hours of the day.

The distinction just made, is a fundamental one for clear understanding.

Of all the many civilizations that preceded our own,

the oldest one of which we are aware that studied the true meaning of dreams were the Egyptians. Documentation dating back more than 4000 years confirming this fact is kept in the British Museum in London. Both the Egyptians and the Assyrians were masters of the art of dream interpretation. Then, only 500 years ago, Nostradamus refined and extended through his own work the understanding of the meaning behind the images seen in our sleep.

Images are also sometimes called *the universal language*, and it is through them that communication takes place between the invisible plane and our world of matter. It is for this reason, that true dreams can only be conceived during nocturnal sleep. They derive from the eternal world, which is a higher part of Creation, and can only be apprehended through natural, living symbols, according to Nature's Laws which are under the command of the Creator.

Nostradamus mastered this Law and he was thus able to use symbolism to explain the meaning behind our dreams.

If a solid foundation in the form of an understanding of the Governing Laws, the so-called 'Blueprint' from the Master, the laid foundation since the beginning, is lacking, how can we hope to build a solid structure upon it, organizing our discoveries in the way intended?

You may have found books that purport to be about dreams in which the author would have you believe, that the idea that dreams contain meaningful symbols is nothing more than an ancient superstition, one that we in our modern era should have outgrown; or, on the other hand, that what symbols mean is something that changes and develops as society itself changes. If the latter is the case, how is it, that living symbols such as those of a tree or a flower, which are always present in nature, never change? Has the rose, the queen of flowers, or its exquisite design, changed to suit the times? It is a Law that nature speaks to us in the Universal Language of Symbols. No doubt, if man knew how to change the innermost heart of God's Creation, he would have done so long ago. The very structure of mother nature speaks to us through all the living symbols we enjoy in our precious life—and thank heaven it cannot be changed by anyone, because it outlives us through space and time. *Nature's Law is the Manifestation of the Will of the Creator.*

That same Law speaks to us in the form of pictures we receive in sleep: what is really meant by the word '*Dream*'. Only we humans, with our Soul/Spirit, can benefit from that privilege of receiving messages from beyond through living symbols and thus allow the understanding of them to affect our present and future. Our sleep provides us with a natural means to prepare ourselves for what is to come, provided, that we want to let it happen.

It is important that at the end of the day we should prepare for sleep by putting aside our preoccupation with the events of the day and not dwell on unfinished business. Free your mind of all worries; leave them on your desk in the office, or lock them up in your file cabinet, then close the door—don't think about them. Your mind will thank you for unburdening it in the evening hours at least. Reorient, by surrounding yourself with beautiful and harmonious stimuli that will quickly put you into a relaxed, peaceful and humble mood. For instance, any form related to art that requires Soul involvement; or simply let silence reign; or soak yourself in classical music. When you do so, you are enabling your antenna to adjust to a different range of channels from the environment than you usually absorb by thinking. Such a process is necessary to activate our deep interior feelings and to set the intuitive faculty free from the intellect so that it can work undisturbed. When we turn our thoughts then in gratitude toward our Creator, they can also travel with us when we leave behind the day and enter the world of sleep. We pass through several stages until we fall into *deep sleep*, or what science calls Rapid Eye Movement (REM) sleep.

My choice of the word 'fall' is deliberate, because everyone, I am sure, has had the experience of feeling as if they are falling while drifting into deep sleep. The body may even react with a convulsion. That moment is the one at which the two parts that are active in us, the mind and the Soul, change the priority of their respective activities.

The moment the Soul drifts off into the eternal world and arrives at a region of its origin, we can obtain messages concerning our life here on earth in the symbolic language of images. That 'sneak preview' should support and reassure us in our immediate plans and help us in the decisions we have to make every day. It can confirm that prosperous, joyful times are ahead or, on the contrary, warn us of the difficult times that are inevitable in everyone's life. If we know what is imminent, we can prepare ourselves for it, and manage it better when it arrives, than we would have done otherwise. Through the exercise of our *Free Will* one has the opportunity to change course and either prevent unpleasant surprises or fully enjoy the good fortunes to come.

Let me give you an example of how helpful images seen in our sleep can be, if we pay attention to their message and do not ignore their purposeful significance.

I'd like to share with you an incident that occurred recently within my own family.

On a Sunday at the end of November, around noon, I returned home from a brief outing to find my husband leaning over the kitchen table with his head down, as if accepting a terrible defeat. I had never seen him in such a condition.

"What's wrong with you?" I asked.

"I don't feel well," he said.

I saw that his face was pale. "You look awful."

"I'm in severe pain," he replied. Then he gasped for air.

"Where does it hurt?"

He pointed to his stomach. Oh well, I thought, he must have eaten something that disagreed with him, and got food poisoning as a result, or perhaps he was simply constipated.

After he had replied negatively to all of my 'common sense' questions, I suggested that he let me take him to the hospital. "No," he said, "I'll wait for a while, it should get better," thus confirming in my mind his stubbornness, always thinking he knows best.

"Come on, let's go," I urged him, "I can drive you to emergency, they're open on Sunday."

"No," he insisted, "I'm just going to lie down for a while."

So be it then, I thought, and went upstairs to make his bed.

As I ascended the stairs, I remembered a dream I had three days before, in which I had seen an old house burning.

When I looked it up in Nostradamus' *Interpretations*, I read that such an image indicated "unexpected death, losing your lover."

Immediately I sensed a connection with my husband's condition, turned on my heels and rushed back down stairs.

"Quick, we're going to the hospital. Now!"

"No," he complained, "I don't want to go."

Well, it was time to take command. I screamed at him, "Hurry up! Quick! It could be your heart! (That's what I guessed it was.)

Finally I got him into the car and we sped off.

"Slow down," he said, "I'm getting dizzy..."

Oh no, I thought, if I don't make it in time... He moved his fingers. "Are they getting numb?"

"Yes."

Then I knew it was, indeed, a heart attack. I stepped on the gas pedal, God help me, I thought, I must reach the hospital, what if he collapses next to me now...

We arrived at the emergency ward. There wasn't a wheelchair in sight, he could hardly remain on his feet, and there was no one at reception. I remember hitting the little bell and hearing a voice telling me to fill in the forms.

"Fill in the forms?!" I repeated incredulously. "Get

moving, woman! This man is having a heart attack! Move, move!"

She ran off and returned with a wheelchair, and wheeled him to the area behind the curtains.

Ten minutes later I was in a chair beside his bed. The activity of three doctors and two nurses around him and the sight of him connected to the monitoring equipment gave me the impression of a situation of extreme urgency.

And how right it turned out I was. One of the doctors approached me, and looked at me silently for a while.

"Is it over?" I asked. "Is he through?"

"Oh no," he replied. "It just hit. It's a heart attack—a severe one. Thank you so much for bringing him in at the right time. Minutes later, it would have been too late. He wouldn't have made it."

It's not me you have to thank, I thought to myself, my feeling catching up to me as I silently sent my heartfelt thanks to heaven.

I was fully aware that by my decision to act quickly I had invoked destiny, and that action in turn had been prompted by the warning received through my dream. In such communications between the next world and this world of matter, our earth, we can recognize the Creator's love for humanity. This is the love that allows us to antici-pate, through dreams, the otherwise unexpected daily occurrences of life.

After three weeks in the hospital and a successful triple bypass, my husband was released two days before Christmas. Our whole family was reunited and we never experienced the true sense of Christmas as the celebration of *divine love* more, than we did that year.

Poets and Philosophers have also discussed in their written works the promising, comforting fountains of the realm we enter during sleep, where only 'golden dreams' smile and wait for us which confirms an old saying:
"All the *good* is coming from above".

Our nightly journey into the eventful world of the beyond, with our personal faculties fully prepared, is the key to our overall well-being, preventing us from 'sleep disorders'. It nourishes the Body and Soul together, maintaining the balance we need, and assuring our inner harmony so we can start refreshed and full of strength the next day.

As you become accustomed not to interfere in the activities of the small (intuitive) brain, you will find it easy to distinguish the dreams to which you should pay attention. Meaningful and valuable dreams are recognizable by the distinctness and clarity of the images in them, without words being spoken. (Remember, in order to speak, we must *produce* words, but our mind is set to be out of order.) I suggest that in the beginning, until you have more experience, you keep a notebook and pen on your night-table. When we wake up, having received and carried the load of information in our dreams, we have to concentrate to retain the images that we saw so vividly only moments before. Write down descriptions of the images that most caught your attention. It is important to try and remain in the half-awake state to facilitate recall of what you have seen and avoid being overwhelmed by the thought that it is time to get up or smelling the freshly brewed coffee and remembering the busy schedule that faces you. Allowing your attention to become thus too quickly focused on waking affairs, interrupts the process of transmission from the subconscious to the active brain. As soon as the intellect becomes occupied with earthly matters, it is difficult to recall your dreams, because waking awareness dominates the mind and overpowers the dream experience. A valuable dream can thus be erased.

I conclude this chapter with a quotation from a well-known Philosopher, C. G. Lichtenberg:

"It belongs to the privilege of every human being, knowing that we dream and having the KNOWLEDGE of it. The dream is part of our life, and should be connected with our daily life in order to become ONE. Only that should we call "REAL LIFE."

DISCOVER THE
SECRETS OF SLEEP

Why do we sleep?

lmost a third of our life is spent in the condition we call 'sleep'. What, though, really happens during that time? Could it be, that what does happen is something unrecognized by many, yet important for all who wish to know more of what it is, that a human being consists of, as well as being vital to our mental and physical health? Considering how much time that amounts to, one is bound to think, 'What a waste!' Yet, without it, of course, we could not exist. The sleep cycle contains the balance between Body and Soul that is necessary for our well being. An advertising slogan for sleeping pills refers to that important balance, and they sell well because millions of people in contemporary society find it difficult to achieve a restful sleep. Why is that?

Let us look more closely at the question of why we sleep.

We human beings are part of, and under the Law of Nature, and like all living creatures participate in the endlessly repeating pattern that is the cycle of life. In the day we respond to the sun's invitation and are active. When, however, the sun goes to sleep, and is replaced in the sky by the moon and stars, the visible circumstances again seem to invite living things to rest and sleep. It is, of course, a natural process, and can be compared with 'changing guards'. The day shift comes to an end, and the mind, intellect, departs to take rest. The night shift begins, when the new guard guides the Human Spirit to the realm of beauty and harmony, where our 'dream world' awaits us. Most of us take sleep for granted and dismiss it in simple terms of sleeping after becoming tired.

Sleep is not necessary for the body, however; for it, when tired, merely resting is sufficient. Yet we know from experience that if we only rested without sleeping, we would not last very long. The energy that is so crucial for continuing to live and act is not replenished by only resting the body. We need to sleep, to "recharge" our mental as well as our physical part, to produce in our overall condition an equilibrium, as in the balancing of scales.

Let me use a simple comparison: that of a car.

Every component of a car is an example of technology engineered in the finest details in the mind of the inventor, as part of a comprehensive design, with its own place and purpose, and connected to all the other parts in specific and intentional ways. The omission of any one part would cause the whole to be incomplete, so that, quite simply, it could not work. The motor, the gas, the oil, the sparkplugs, and any number of other necessary things could be present;

but still, the car would not run and would not move.

To get the car started in the customary fashion, we must first turn the key in the switch, causing the spark-plugs to ignite. The energy necessary for turning on the motor is thus produced, and the car is consequently pre-pared to be set in motion.

Let us apply this scheme analogically to the human body.

All living creatures, let us remember—and, indeed, the whole of Creation—exist under a uniform higher Law. Every organ of our body is masterfully designed by our Creator, put in place and assigned a special function; and its successful performance of this function is connected to and dependent on the other organs. Just as with the car, leaving out one part of the mechanism or one organ of the body would deprive the whole of the essential characteristic of completeness, and thus interrupt the harmonious action of the whole and, ultimately, cause it to fail altogether.

The heart (our motor) and the blood (our fuel) would be in place; but still, that heart would not be beating, and nothing in the body would be moving. To set the bodily mechanism in motion, the switch in us has to be turned on, *igniting the spark* in us! Our Spirit (so-called sparkplug) is the assigned distribution centre for the heavenly fuel, the driving force, the energy necessary for our heart, the motor in our system, that is then activated allowing our entire body to begin to fully function and move.

If we fail to maintain either of those two all-important

sources of power in us, namely Body and Spirit neglecting either and not taking proper care of it, our affected motor will eventually run dry and the result will be a breakdown that can shorten our life span. The heart and all our other organs will become unbalanced in their working. One way this can happen is through paying attention exclusively to the physical body's needs; failing to nurture our Spirit will ultimately cause a major interruption, leading to discomfort, weakness, illness and, even, collapse.

The invisible source inside us, comprising of the Spirit and Soul, can only be felt; it is what people mean when they speak of their 'deepest feelings' known as 'gut feelings', and also 'first impressions'—an invisible language, that reaches us intuitively before the mind consciously registers anything. The emotions we feel are an expression only of the Soul, whereas any physical pain we feel results from bodily injury.

We are thus confronted with two different sources of individual function. Emotions occur suddenly as a result of devastating personal impacts, or, on the other hand, overwhelming joy touching us and shaking our innermost selves. Great joy expressed in laughter, or tears running down the cheeks, are only some of the sensations expressed through the Soul's inner sensitivity. Try as we might, we can never command ourselves to be emotional, because it is something that takes place without the participation of the mind. It is in the other side of our interior being, the invisible but very much alive one, where emotions have their deep arising.

The brain immediately registers the signals radiating from the Soul and transmits them to the appropriate cellular area of itself, and the physical reaction then occurs, whether it is a flow of tears, a wave of goosebumps on our body for a few moments, uncontrollable trembling, or what we refer to as heartfelt laughter and so on. When we speak of 'a good-hearted person', we really mean *a good soul*. The heart is only an organ required to pump blood through our veins. The same applies to our other organs, which all have special and unique roles assigned to them by the Creator in view of the environment, the earth, our home, in which we live.

What does all of this have to do with why we sleep?

The foregoing facts are those I consider necessary in order to be able to understand how the two sides of our being complement and support each other. Our physical body, with all of its functioning organs in place, only provides temporary shelter for the Spirit during our lifetime. In our earthly environment, communication therefore can only be established through radiation: and that Spirit-Radiation in us is, what we call 'Soul'. That necessary adjustment, which takes place through divine Law, is a manifestation of the 'living code' required for the Spirit to be effective in the world of matter.

Let me summarize it in simple words.

Our Spirit, in being covered or 'dressed up' in different layers of matter, is complying with the 'dress code', according to our 'Master's (God's) Blueprint', required for life on earth. Doing so enables the Spirit to radiate what is known to us as Soul, in the form of communicating through our 'deep inner feelings.' That God-given instrument is the fundamental igniting spark in us.

When we recognize and practice these facts of life by giving our Soul priority in the actions we take, we hold the living key for success and happiness and our well being as a whole in our own hands. Through a gentle flow of proper conduct and behavior, we can shape and direct 'destiny'. For instance, we can begin practicing on this gentle human path, starting within the smallest union, what we call 'our family life.' It would spread automatically into our community, becoming stronger and stronger, which will affect the whole nation to a point, where the whole world can adopt it and rise to a long desired, harmonious and peaceful place.

What are we waiting for?

That is exactly what our Creator had in mind, in granting us the connecting tool, namely our Spirit to use, participating in a united way in effort to maintain this beautiful earth, in showing gratitude for our allowed short passing through.

Let us move on to the Soul and Spirit, understanding each as occupying its rightful place and performing its assigned activity. If we understand why we have them in the first place, clarity will emerge concerning the purpose of sleeping. We have always taken the Soul and Spirit for granted, and talk about them incessantly—but where are they? Lets find out.

When we speak of a 'high in Spirit' person, it conjures in our mind a picture of a well educated individual, especially one with a talent for expressing ideas brilliantly or, with a talent of intellectual wit. But is he really high in Spirit? Or would it be more accurate to describe him as smart or well educated? Since the Spirit has not a visible substance, let me quote the Author of *In the Light of Truth*, the 'Grail-Message'.

> *"The Spirit is not wit and not intellect. Nor is it acquired knowledge. It is erroneous, therefore, to call a person 'rich in spirit' because he has studied, read and observed much and knows how to converse well about it. Spirit is something entirely different. It is an independent consistency, coming from the world of its homogeneous species, which is different from the part to which the earth and thus the physical body belong. The spiritual world lies higher, it forms the upper and highest part of Creation. Spirit has nothing to do with the earthly intellect, only with the quality that is described as 'deep inner feeling'. To be rich in spirit, therefore, is the same as 'having deep inner feelings'."*

Let us apply these facts in our discussion of sleep.

Our body needs to come to a state of total relaxation, which is only possible in a horizontal position. We put body and mind at rest, and on a 'low energy' setting. The radiation of the body consequently declines. Do we not automatically put a blanket on a sleeping person, knowing that they could easily become cold? These are the signs of the Soul loosening its firm union with the body in order to be able to drift off to the eternal world, its region of origin. If the Soul/Spirit severed, rather than only loosened, its connection with the body, death would take place. It is for this reason that sleep is sometimes called by science 'the little brother of death'. We are, are we not, all aware that there is no guarantee, that when we go to sleep in the evening we will wake up in the morning? It would be a great step forward then, for us to hold account for our activities of that day, to examine silently before our conscience, if we have done 'our best', so that no shadows linger around us. Through that clear self-acknowledgement we are purified within, and thus prepare and assure our Soul of a carefree and enlightened journey into the spiritual realm from which it came.

We pass through several stages during sleep, until we enter 'deep sleep' where we can bathe in the fountain of youth. The confirmation of this process is especially visible to us when we look in the mirror in the morning. The wrinkles (if you had some!) from the evening before, perhaps even many of them and deeply engraved, have evened out and have almost disappeared. Your face might have a kind of serene glow, nourished in youth, provided of course, that you had truly rested in a 'deep sleep'. A confirmation can be found in an old saying, "Sleep makes you beautiful!" If you want to test it, see if you can accomplish the same results by simply resting for the same length of time. Your reflection in the mirror will show you a different result. You will undoubtedly see a face even more drained, and the appearance of wrinkles unchanged.

We can even observe on the face of a sleeper the different stages being reached, with the face relaxing, the whole demeanour changing, the chin dropping—and the snore beginning. Then we can be assured that the person is well and truly 'out', as we call it, when even a slamming door cannot wake them up. Deep sleep is that referred to by science as REM, or Rapid Eye Movement sleep. Studies have confirmed that in that stage of sleep, with the eyelids closed, the mind is no longer in control, the body is at complete rest, and yet the eyeballs are in constant movement. It was found that, when the individual was dreaming of climbing a ladder, their eyes looked up; when picking something up from the floor, they looked down, and so on. In other words, they witnessed living events in that stage of sleep, precisely the one that leads us to the world of dreams.

Let me summarize in simple words.

During sleep, the Soul is set free to escape, in a natural manner, to the region of its origin, which exists in a higher level of Creation, in order to receive there the nutrition it requires, in other words being 'recharged'. This infusion of nourishment is a major aspect of our sleep process.

The degree and quality of the strength we absorb on our nocturnal journey depends on the preparation we have ourselves made, in the sense of the depth of sincerity, humility and purity we realize within us, before going to sleep and most of all, don't forget, we need to eliminate our 'constant worrisome, nagging mind' to avoid indigestion.

Perhaps we are now more able to answer the question, "Why is it, that so many millions of people in our materialistically oriented society have such difficulty finding refuge in a well deserved *good night's sleep*?" It is, that our awareness of our most precious gift from our Creator, the Spirit in us, which confer life, has dwindled to nothing: we have ignored it, and forgotten it, and neglected to take care of it.

When we wake up in the morning, Body and Soul once again merge into their firm union to produce a fully functioning human being with the strength to deal with the newly arisen day. All who enjoy a 'good night's sleep' experience tremendous energy, with joy and confidence to face what may come. In contrast are those who struggle to get their night's rest and are miserable in the morning, feeling weak and without drive or ambition. There is much truth in the saying, when referring to such people, He is not quite himself, or, She isn't 'together'! Such people's 'scale' is not balanced. We are responsible for paying attention to our condition when it is such, and not doing so can have negative consequences. An imbalance of the Body and Soul leads to disharmony, unhappiness, depression, illness, and even collapse. Therefore, we have our own well being in our own hands.

What a support and gift of love our Creator gave us, in

this ability to achieve, through practice, a higher level of Spiritual Realization! Everyone is able to benefit equally by drawing from the highest founts of strength and beauty through our Spirit; or, on the other hand, ignoring it, with the attendant consequences. How many in our present time, through ignorance (or willful ignorance), fail to recognize *the importance and vital purpose of Sleep!*

NOSTRADAMUS'

Egyptian Dream Interpretation Book

German Edition
1928

Nostradamus' Egyptian Dream Interpretation Book

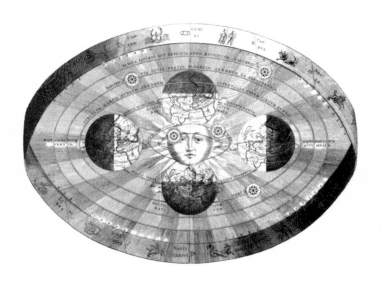

DREAM SYMBOLOGY

*Analisation and meaning
of images seen in your Dreams*

Abbess, to see a female abbot:
  *haughtiness and arrogance are detrimental to your
  character.*

Abbot, to see one in his robes:
  means annoyance.

Abundance, to experience:
  you are holding onto false hopes.

Abduction, being or witnessing:
  an unexpected, imminent marriage.

Accident:
  relief from worries.

Accusation, being accused by others:
  restlessness and discontent.

Accusing others:
  troubled success.

Acorns, gather:
  means profit.

Acorn, receiving a wreath of acorn leaves:
  distinction and honour.

Acquainted, getting to know someone:
there will be a loss or affliction.

Adder, seeing this kind of snake:
an unpleasant and dangerous acquaintance.

Adultery committing:
Horrendous disagreements

Adultery, withstanding the temptation of:
triumph over your enemies.

Advertisement, seeing the ad:
you will fall into disgrace.

Advertisement or public notification:
work without success.

Advice, giving advice to others:
luck in completing difficult business matters.

Advice, receiving:
you will be deceived.

Air balloon, to see one flying:
a separation ahead.

Alcoholic, being one:
happiness and health.

Almonds, eating them:
your nosiness will embarrass you.

Aloe, seeing this plant:
you will renew an old friendship.

Altar, to see one:
comfort and enjoyment.

Amber, seeing this stone as a necklace:
receiving a gift.

Ambush, falling into an ambush trap:
hardship in business.

Amusement park:
you will be well and enjoy advantages.

Anchor, to see one:
  confirmation of hopes.

Anchor, to throw one:
  great danger.

Anchovy, eating or seeing:
  good consistent luck.

Angel, seeing:
  good luck, confirmation of hopes and wishes,
  receiving news which will please you.

Angel, to become one:
  means great honour, for a sick person it means death.

Angry, to become:
  irreconcilable enemies.

Animals, belonging to you or feeding them:
  happiness and wealth.

Animals, seeing various breeds:
  associations with unknown people.

Animals being tamed:
  patiently overcoming obstacles.

Animals jumping:
  loss of freedom or independence.

Antler, to see these:
  faithlessness and treason.

Ants, to see them:
  much work; achievements recognized and honoured.

Ant hill, stepping on one:
  you will find yourself in bad company.

Anvil, seeing one:
  a steady job and secure income.

Apostle, to see or speak to one:
  receiving good news.

Apple, to see or eat an exquisite one:
joy, amusement, long life, good fortune in love, stead-fastness and good luck in business matters.

Apple, cutting a tasty apple:
separation from your boyfriend or girlfriend.

Apple, eating a sour one:
disputes, arguments, sadness, or false friends.

Apple, seeing many on a tree:
you will have many relatives.

Apple juice, or drinking apple wine:
efforts in vain, arguments, indecency.

Apricots seeing or eating:
a late marriage for you.

April Fool's Day:
you will experience honour in the near future.

Apron, putting on a beautiful one:
you will receive presents.

Apron, made of silk:
fortunate money circumstances.

Arbour, being under one:
a pleasant acquaintance will come your way.

Archery, to span and shoot:
comfort in your sorrow.

Archbishop, to see one:
abrupt death.

Architect, being on a building site:
forthcoming danger.

Architect, to see one giving instructions:
confirms a well-managed life.

Argument, occurring between friends:
declining prosperity.

Argument, winning in one:
with great effort, your status will improve.

Argument, with boy or girl friend:
an advantageous marriage.

Ark, seeing one:
you will become annoyed.

Arm, being broken:
disaster or death.

Arm, being hairy:
a huge fortune.

Arm, being wounded:
indicates sadness.

Arm, having a huge one:
hard work ahead.

Arm, having a small one:
falling into poverty.

Arm bandage, to put one or several on:
means sickbed.

Armchair:
a comfortable and amusing life.

Armour, to wear:
stay away from your enemies.

Arms, seeing many of them:
conditions will worsen; great unhappiness.

Arms and weapons, being broken:
a dispute will occur.

Arms and weapons, to see or own them:
happiness and honour.

Arms or weapons, being made:
bad times are ahead.

Army, to see one in combat:
misery and grief.

Army, to see one marching:
mischief and harm approaching.

Arrested, being arrested yourself:
obstacles in ventures, fraud and slander.

Arrow, to see one:
forthcoming hardship, disagreements.

Arrow, shooting:
you will steer yourself into bad luck.

Arsenal, to see one:
war times approaching, unrest.

Artichoke, seeing or eating:
secretly suffering, imminent separation.

Ashes, to see:
a bitter delusion or insult.

Asparagus, eating or seeing:
flourishing ventures, trust enjoying.

Asparagus field:
huge gain or profit.

Assets:
forthcoming losses.

Audience, having one with a dignitary:
happiness and gain.

Authority, seeing a person of authority:
bad luck and a lengthy lawsuit.

Avalanche, to witness one:
affliction and grief.

Awaken, to see yourself awaken exceptionally early:
happiness and forthcoming wealth.

Axe, to see one:
a rebellion, revolt, or bad luck in general.

Axe, to split wood with one:
means a separation, being apart.

Bacon (ham, smoked meat), eating or seeing:
death of a friend or relative, pursuit by enemies.

Badger, catching:
loosing your living quarters.

Bagpipe playing, hearing:
joyfulness..

Bag (paper), seeing many:
unfaithfulness.

Bailiff, seeing or talking to:
*warning about bad people, difficulty in keeping the first
lover; being tricked in business matters.*

Baked-goods, eating:
forthcoming harm or troubles.

Baker or bakery, seeing:
a blessed year.

Baking bread:
good nutritious food enjoying.

Baking cookies:
to become useful to others.

Bake (kneading) trough, empty one seeing:
misery will come your way.

Bake (kneading) trough, full one seeing:
means great wealth.

Baker's oven:
good fortune.

Bald, being:
you are reaching old age.

Bald-headed person:
derision, scorn.

Ball playing:
  good prospect.

Ball-hitting:
  continuous disagreements.

Ball (dance), attending:
  extraordinary good luck, great honour.

Ballet seeing:
  deception and cheating.

Balloon seeing:
  misfortune lies ahead.

Balcony, standing on:
  reciprocate love.

Balsam, having it:
  earning praise.

Bandit, seeing:
  means persecution.

Bang-noise, explosion:
  an ill-fated message.

Banishing someone:
  bad luck ahead.

Bank-building:
  a flourishing business, security in ventures.

Banker, seeing:
  involvement in gossip.

Barefooted running:
  body weakness, or misfortune

Barley, eating:
  good health.

Barley, seeing:
  food shortage and worries.

Barn, empty seeing:
  being disappointed in your hopes.

Barn, full, seeing:
  sudden, unexpected wealth.

Barracks, seeing:
  assurance in behavior and attitude.

Barrel, seeing:
  beware of gluttony.

Barrier-gate, breaking:
  returning from abroad.

Basin, in brass or copper:
  faithfulness, loyalty.

Basin, washing yourself:
  cleanliness is the essence of health.

Basket, empty seeing:
  indicates losses.

Basket, a closed one:
  keeping secrets.

Basket (with handle) carrying:
  worries about the future.

Basket with flowers:
  lucky in love.

Bat, catching:
  for ill persons, a quick recovery

Bat, seeing:
  doubtful business success; inconsistent people around you.

Bathing, and not perspire:
  interruptions in business.

Bathtub water, muddy:
  danger of fire.

Bathing, in clear water:
  happiness, health, luck and success in love.

Bathing, in muddy water:
  sorrow, ill-health, bad luck and disappointment.

Bathing, in warm water:
ill-person, health; healthy person, obstacles in business.

Bathing, in general:
indicates anger.

Bathing, in the room:
grief, sorrow.

Battle (fight), attending:
means seduction.

Bay-leaf tree:
success in your endeavor.

Bay-leaf picking:
hopes fading away.

Bay-leaf wreath:
coming to honour.

Beans, eating or seeing:
dispute ahead, experiencing misfortune and defamation of character.

Beans seeing in full bloom:
a wish coming true.

Beans, growing:
a purpose is acknowledged.

Beans, being burned:
many annoyances.

Beans, peeling:
worries about the future.

Beans, planting:
a new business takeover.

Bears, seeing:
suffer from injustice, bad gossip (in general, image is not good; furthermore, dreams with hyenas, tigers and wild beasts mean misfortune, quarrels, discord).

Beard, black, good looking:
indicates health.

Beard, grey:
ill-humour, melancholy.

Beard, long one:
profit and luck.

Beard, red:
having false friends.

Beard, seeing on a woman:
annoyance, unpleasantness.

Beard shaving off or taking off:
losses of all kinds, multiple misfortunes.

Beast, predacious animal:
beware of deceitful behaviour.

Beast, being beaten or attacked by one:
quarrel occurring around you.

Bed, a beautiful one:
happiness and good harmony in your marriage.

Bed, not clean; uncomfortable:
you are unsociable and incompatible.

Bed of feathers/comforter or quilt, shaking, in the sun:
family welfare.

Bed, burning:
disaster, illness, death.

Beds, rain falling onto:
excessiveness.

Bed, warmer, warm bottle:
soon to be married.

Bee, seeing:
always a good omen.

Bee, swarm:
confusing matters, complications.

Bee, being stung:
imminent bad luck, disagreements with friends.

Bees, being very busy:
getting on and living well.

Bee honey, collecting honey from the combs:
passing on good advice.

Bees, gathered on a tree:
strengthening love and fidelity.

Bee hive, seeing:
delight and benefits.

Beef, cut up, seeing:
receiving inheritance.

Beef, raw:
(see Meat)

Beer (cloudy) drinking or seeing:
illness and annoyance.

Beer (clear) drinking or seeing:
steady health, cheerfulness and friendly meetings.

Beer, spilling over:
indicates declining wealth.

Beer-barrel:
business is taking off well.

Beer-house, pub:
beware of carelessness.

Beer mug (tankard), seeing:
drinking is harmful.

Beet, turnip:
happy family, prosperity, luck in love.

Beet, field:
huge fortune ahead.

Beet-root, lots seeing:
getting into bigger ventures.

Beet-root, nice, seeing a field:
positive development of your plans.

Beheaded, seeing yourself:
fear, affliction, loss of an influential sponsor.
Beheaded, seeing:
overcoming enemies; return of a long missing friend.
Bell, seeing:
ventures with risk.
Bell-tower, seeing:
happiness, power, honour.
Bells, hearing them ring:
for business: a good omen for received contracts.
for married couple: arguments, disagreement.
Belly, a big one:
being well-off, comfort.
Belly, small:
long-lasting lawsuit.
Belly, swollen:
misfortune, hidden secrets.
Bellows:
squabble, discord.
Belt, finding:
gaining trust.
Belt, in silver:
confined wealth.
Belt, losing:
neglected plans.
Belt, or leash, in gold seeing:
great riches and health.
Belt, tearing apart:
disaster ahead.
Belt, new, wearing:
forthcoming honour, soon to be engaged.
Bench, seeing:
leading a peaceful life.

Bending down:
degradation, harm.

Berries, eating or looking for:
hardship and grief.

Bet, propose one, or agreeing to one:
uncertainty in business; losses ahead.

Betting:
beware of risky speculation.

Bigger becoming, seeing yourself growing huge:
a rich marriage.

Bile, vomiting:
anger, annoyance.

Bill, accounting for:
take good care of your documents.

Billiards, pool playing or seeing:
doubtful venture, inconstancy.

Binding, something:
lawsuit matters.

Birds, singing:
joy with your children, your loved ones seem to be happy.

Birds, flying:
continuation in business, prosperous success.

Bird, in cage:
secure assets.

Birds, colorful or strange, seeing:
vulnerability in relations, concerning your friends.

Bird's nest, finding:
experiencing plenty of joy.

Bird's nest, empty:
annoyance, tricks.

Bird's nest, taking eggs from:
grief and trouble in your daily life.

Nostradamus' Egyptian Dream Interpretation Book

Birth (giving) seeing:
difficulties, trouble.

Birth giving (a happy one), being present:
joy, happiness.

Birth, with complications, attending:
losses, painful disgrace.

Birth, giving to a boy:
prosperity in all undertakings.

Birth, giving to a girl:
painful experiences when you are in a cheerful, joyful mood.

Bishop seeing:
means favoured by a dignitary.

Bite, to fear from an animal, or to escape from:
indicates jealousy.

Bleaching something, seeing or doing:
you will get justification.

Bleeding:
falling into sadness.

Blessing, receiving:
joy and happiness.

Blind, becoming:
danger ahead.

Blind, being:
deceived by false friends.

Blind people, leading:
taking opportunities to help the needy.

Blind people, seeing:
a hindrance, obstacles in undertakings.

Blinking-eye, seeing:
huge winnings.

Blisters, tearing off the Band-Aid:
good health.

Block (log), hitting:
someone insults you.

Blood, dripping from you to the ground:
a good omen.

Blood collecting, picking up:
also a good sign.

Blood drinking:
is good.

Blood, rotten, foul, seeing:
indicates severe illness.

Blood, being carried:
is malicious and evil.

Blood collecting from an animal:
indicates big business ambition.

Blood, seeing curdled:
indicates illness.

Blood seeing of a nice color:
cheerfulness in the days to come.

Blood, vomiting:
wealth for those who are poor.

Blueberries, eating:
struggling future ahead.

Boar, seeing:
being frightened; being followed by rivals.

Boar, seeing destroying crops:
dispute with friends.

Boar, to kill—shoot:
victory over a rival, overcoming danger.

Boar-wild, being attacked:
being held-up by evil people.

Board-game, playing or seeing:
uncertainty and doubtful success in business deals.

Boarder, making or establishing:
money situation is improving.

Boards, seeing:
flourishing business.

Boat, small:
a forthcoming trip.

Boat, ferry, riding in, on sea or river, in clear water:
joy and success in all undertakings.

Boat sinking:
breakup of a love relationship.

Body deformation:
you will be shamed.

Body, injuring:
being in trouble.

Body, your own, exposing:
experiencing shame.

Bolt (lock, deadbolt), seeing:
secretly annoyed.

Bone marrow, finding in legs:
great wealth and happiness.

Bone marrow (dumpling), preparing:
making a good living.

Bones, seeing:
lots of work ahead.

Bones, nibbling on:
worries about food shortage

Bonnet, putting on:
soon to be married.

Bonnet and hats, seeing:
lingering disease.

Boot, good quality and nice looking:
coming to honour, loyal servants.

Books buying:
usefulness to yourself and others.

Books, learning from:
earning respect.

Books, seeing:
experiencing the unexpected.

Books, seeing being burned:
hope for joy diminishing.

Books, useful ones, reading:
a private speculation

Borrowing:
free yourself of worrisome matters.

Born, being:
for a needy person, good; for a well-off person, bad.

Bottles, broken:
indicates sadness.

Bottles, cleaning:
being involved with bad company.

Bottle, seeing or having:
joy and fun.

Bottom (buttocks), seeing your own:
confusion in business.

Bottom, seeing of a woman:
succumb to trivial matters, or a silly fuss.

Bow, knot:
slipping into difficult situations.

Bowl, dish, seeing:
dinner invitation.

Box, seeing:
discovering a secret.

Box, losing:
disagreement with yourself.

Box, in silver, seeing:
good omen.

Box, painted beautiful:
lots of fun.

Box, with a portrait:
to soon have a pleasant acquaintance.

Box-tree, shrub, seeing green:
affirmation of your hopes.

Boys, seeing:
addition to the family.

Bracelets putting on:
a secret love.

Bracelets, getting as a gift:
a returning love.

Braided hair:
soon to be united in love.

Branches, green:
your hopes are coming true.

Brandy, spirits, drinking or seeing:
evil lust.

Brass, merchandise, seeing:
being cheated by someone.

Bread baking:
your undertakings are ending well.

Bread burned, seeing:
means irresponsibility.

Bread eating:
having loyal friends and gaining more.

Bread, eating while still warm:
becoming sick.

Bread seeing turning bad:
varying, inconsistent luck.

Bread, being prepared:
for diligent people, good; lazy ones, bad.

Bread, seeing a nice loaf:
to receive honour and wealth.

Breast, exposing:
bashfulness, modesty.

Breast, big and healthy:
enjoying sturdy health.

Breast, seeing, nursing a baby:
joy in your marriage.

Breast, seeing a woman's:
continuance being in love.

Breast, hairy, seeing:
lots of happiness in love.

Bricklayer, seeing:
laziness brings harm.

Bride seeing, running:
indicates death.

Bride or groom, hugging:
being faithful, even at a far distance

Bride or groom, escorting to the altar:
peace of mind.

Bridge, walking or driving over:
happiness in love and all ventures.

Bridge, walking under:
lots of obstacles but still reaching the goal.

Bridge, seeing:
secure undertakings.

Bridge, seeing, being built of stone:
durability in actions and proceedings.

Bridge, seeing, being built of wood:
insupportable, destruction of hopes and actions.

Bridge, seeing, collapsing:
big interruptions in business.

Bristles, seeing:
there are obstacles in your ventures.

Broom:
unpleasantness and difficulties among friends.

Brother or sister, talking or seeing:
annoyance, disagreements.

Brother, seeing him walk away (death image):
diminishing of a powerful enemy.

Brother, saying farewell to him:
sadness, depression.

Broth, drinking or eating:
good proceedings in business; for a ill person, a slow recovery; Lovers will soon tie the knot.

Broken pieces:
all earthly things are transient.

Brushing:
lots of fun to come.

Buck, rammler killing:
defeat of enemies.

Buckle:
continuation in business ventures.

Building, seeing one being demolished:
brushing obstacles aside.

Building, nice and large:
new ventures, undertakings.

Building, small living in:
peace of mind with your destiny.

Buffalo, seeing:
many casualties, losses.

Bull, seeing or being pursued:
risk, loosing a dear friend, unpleasantness from family members.

Bullet, being hit:
you will need doctor's care.

Bullets, rolling in front of you:
ill-fated success.

Bullets, flying into your house:
danger lies ahead.

Bumps on your body, swollen:
getting real estate.

Burden, heavy:
depression.

Burdock sticking on you:
warning of obtrusive people.

Buried being alive:
coming into great danger.

Buried, seeing yourself:
health and long life.

Burial watching:
sorrow, discord, illness or disease.

Burning, seeing:
forthcoming disaster.

Burning glass, looking through:
errors, mistakes.

Bushes, cutting up:
out of love, you remove all obstacles.

Bushes (underbrush), seeing:
expect obstacles.

Bushes, hiding behind:
danger at present.

Businessman, seeing:
good progress in ventures.

Butcher, seeing or talking:
being offended, loosing your lover, rejection.

Butter, eating:
discord, conflict, annoyance with relatives.

Butter, making:
inner calmness.

Butterfly, seeing or catching:
unsteadiness, unfaithfulness.

Buying something:
extravagance brings disadvantage.

Cabbage, seeing or eating:
unexpected grief, sorrow.

Cabbage leaves, Savoy, seeing or eating:
pretending happiness, showing off.

Cabinet-maker, or visiting cabinet-makers shop:
discord in your matters, cleaning up.

Cage, cleaning out:
imprisonment, or other danger.

Cage, emptying of birds:
release of affliction.

Cake (torte), fancy:
revelry is harming your health.

Cake, baking:
happiness, prosperity.

Calculate, without reading a result:
annoyance, cheating.

Calendar, seeing:
achieving a better living standard.

Calves, seeing:
unwise tricks.

Calves, being killed:
recovery from illness.

Camel, seeing:
experiencing something out of the ordinary; becoming rich.

Camomile, seeing:
you will live to an old age.

Can (jug):
good news.

Can (jug), drinking from:
means joy.

Can (watering):
(see watering can).

Canary, seeing or hearing:
empty compliments.

Candlelight:
being spared trouble.

Candles, blowing out:
a break up with an acquaintance..

Candles, burning, carrying:
indicates death.

Candles, seeing:
invitation to a happy occasion.

Cannon ball, seeing:
experiencing sorrow.

Cannon discharge:
withstanding something repulsive

Canopy, seeing:
a position of dignity, joy

Cantina-(kitchen) woman, working in, talking or seeing:
late (but not too late), coming out of misery.

Car:
(see Vehicle).

Cardinal:
happiness and welfare.

Card player, seeing:
escaping from danger.

Card playing:
arguments, unhappy in your love, late marriage.

Card playing, with lots of pictures in it:
favourable prospects, rich bride.

Card playing, with lots of hearts in it:
happy, satisfying marriage and many children.

Card tricks:
seeking popularity.

Cargo-wagon:
busy activity in your business.

Carnations:
your descendants bring you lots of joy.

Carp, eating or seeing:
health improvement.

Carpets:
fondness of luxury and waste brings decline in prosperity.

Carriage (coach), riding in:
tendency to be arrogant, will lead to misery.

Carriage (coach), stepping out of it:
loosing your dignitary position.

Carrier-seeing:
anger, discord.

Carrion-animal:
good times, long life.

Case (box), seeing or owing:
stolen goods are being returned.

Cash box, yours, or seeing one:
disadvantage in business.

Cast—wheelbarrow, pulling:
live beyond one's means.

Castle, seeing:
very good, joyful omen.

Castle on fire:
disaster, illness.

Cattle herd, seeing:
prosperity.

Cattle, guiding:
immediate prosperity, then becomes bad luck

Cats seeing:
annoyance, persecution, cheated by lovers, or servants, having contact with false people, and not knowing it.

Cats, being scratched or bitten by:
coming into evil care taking.

Catching:
insidiousness, tricks.

Caterpillar:
damage to your belongings.

Cauliflower:
honour, and profit.

Cave, dying in it:
low in spirit, depression.

Caves, seeing or living in:
big changes in your luck and happiness.

Celery:
beware of flattery.

Cellar, seeing or being in:
sickness lies ahead.

Cellar, sweeping:
bad business.

Cellar steps, falling down:
prolonging disease.

Chain, seeing:
imprisonment, pursuit outwitted by enemies, soon taking your bride to the altar.

Chain, wearing:
bad, disastrous times ahead.

Chain, being chained:
a position is being offered.

Chair, beautiful, seeing:
promotion, high position, wealth.

Chair, dirty and worn out:
interruption or destroying family harmony.

Chair of many colours:
happy times ahead.

Chair in black, seeing:
indicates death.

Chair, sitting in it:
unstable health.

Chalk:
you will lose a lot of money.

Chandelier:
festivities lie ahead.

Chapel, seeing:
joy and loyal friends.

Chaplain, becoming:
great honour.

Charity, handing out:
deep gratitude, calmness, satisfaction.

Charity, receiving:
changing luck.

Charm, being charmed or fascinated:
losing business deals.

Charming someone:
becoming imprudent.

Chasm, seeing, falling into, being swallowed by:
quick rescue from danger.

Cheek:
take more care about cleanliness.

Cheeks, scratched and bony:
sadness and sorrow.

Cheeks, big and red:
  good prospect.
Cherry tree:
  being in a good atmosphere.
Cherries, eating or seeing:
  awkwardness in many things.
Cherries, sour, eating:
  depression, sorrow.
Cheese, eating or seeing:
  happiness and health.
Chess game:
  overall knowledge is the best investment.
Chest (box), empty:
  annoyance, misfortune.
Chest (box), filled:
  plenty, abundance.
Chest-furniture, buying or seeing:
  enduring small losses.
Chest, being wounded:
  for seniors, a bad omen; for youth, a good one.
Child, wrapping nicely up:
  happiness.
Children falling down:
  disruptions, and often decline in business venture.
Children, seeing:
  *joy, health, happiness, inner peace, happy marriage,
  success in all undertakings.*
Children at play:
  joyfulness, cheerfulness, peace of mind.
Childbirth:
  addition to the family, increasing prosperity.
Chimney:
  good family life.

Chimney sweep:
rescue from danger.

China (dishes):
thirst for pleasure is wasting your life away.

Chives:
trouble, damage at your undertakings.

Choking:
you will soon be well.

Christ, worshipping:
indicates joy.

Christ, seeing on the cross:
perish, ruin.

Christ, hearing him speak:
joyfulness.

Church, seeing:
protection from evil and bad things to come.

Church, praying in it:
happiness, joyfulness, progress in all good things.

Church destroyed, or seeing in ruin:
forthcoming disaster.

Churchyard, seeing:
lingering illness, invalidism

Cigar, making:
good health.

Cigar smoking:
enjoyment and wealth.

Circle:
punctuality brings profit in business.

City hall:
involvement in lawsuits.

City, large, walking through it:
vexation of all kinds, restlessness.

City, small and friendly, seeing:
  frugality, making a good living.
City, with many high towers:
  starting a grand operation, enterprise.
City, seeing destroyed:
  misfortune, loss of honour and wealth.
Clergyman, seeing or talking:
  comforting, for the sick or lovers of bad consequences.
Cliff, seeing:
  your calculation is wrong.
Climbing up a hill:
  repulsiveness.
Climbing a tree:
  obtaining honour, dignity, long courtship.
Climbing a mast:
  poverty and affliction.
Clock, seeing:
  being aware of the presence.
Clothing, shabby, wearing:
  poverty.
Closet, seeing:
  sincerity is more pleasing than being reserved.
Clouds, condensed, looking like mountains:
  a oppressive burden.
Clouds, black and heavy:
  discord, arguments, misery.
Clouds, falling down from them:
  huge embarrassment.
Clover, seeing being planted:
  happy family life.
Clover, four-leafed, finding:
  extraordinary luck.

Clover field, lush and green:
hopeful future.

Clyster, seeing:
your business is proceeding well.

Clyster (enema), getting:
riches, wealth.

Clyster (applicator), seeing:
impenetrable business.

Clucking (hen), seeing:
luck and blessings.

Coach (carriage), riding in it:
tendency to haughtiness, sure downfall, misery.

Coach (carriage), stepping out:
losing trust and respectful position.

Coal, seeing:
great wealth, luck.

Coal, seeing burning:
be careful in choosing friends, all in all, carefulness.

Coal, wanted to eat:
misfortune, bad luck.

Coalmine:
marrying a widow.

Coat of Arms:
haughtiness.

Coat, new, putting on:
termination of previous worries.

Coat, too big, putting on:
grief, sadness.

Coat, wearing, or seeing:
blessed with dignity.

Coat, tearing:
separation.

Coat, losing:
   forthcoming misery.
Coat, animal skin, tanner:
   everybody is angry.
Cock (chafer):
   distrust, causing suspicion.
Cockade, seeing or wearing:
   courage, dignified behaviour.
Cockade, not yours, wearing:
   treason and ingratitude.
Coffee, seeing or roasting:
   misfortune, bad luck, persecution.
Coffee grinding:
   annoyance, trouble.
Coffee house, being in it:
   accident of a friend or relative.
Coffin, seeing:
   a long and happy life.
Coins, precious metal:
   considerable riches, lucky business deals.
Colic, having:
   sickness in the family.
Colonnade, seeing, touring, walking:
   riches, happiness.
Color-paint in a box:
   full cash register.
Column (pillar) seeing:
   coming to honour.
Column (pillar), collapsing:
   becoming an invalid; illness.
Comb, seeing:
   illness and worries.

Nostradamus' Egyptian Dream Interpretation Book

Combing hair:
hard, effortless work.

Comedy-(play):
contempt, blasphemy.

Comet, seeing:
price hikes, war, dying and torment, bad harvest,
unexpected news.

Comfort, receiving and not needing it:
good.

Communion (holy) receiving:
steady happiness, finding friends in troublesome times.

Company (get together) in horse-back riding or driving:
tendency for waste and extravagance.

Concert, attending:
grief, loss of relatives and friends.

Confectionery (sweets), eating:
advantage, benefit.

Conference room, court room, attending a public
meeting:
being in pursuit of political activities.

Confessional:
disagreeableness, unpleasantness.

Confessional (priest), seeing or confessing to:
regulating confused business.

Conquest in war:
authority, prestige and honour.

Contrabass, seeing:
dispute, arguments.

Contrabass being played:
unity, harmony.

Convertible (car) driving:
joy and happiness.

Cook, seeing:
  unnecessary expenses.
Cookies, eating:
  means, good times ahead.
Cooking:
  a fun and cheerful festivity lies ahead.
Copper (money):
  effortless work.
Cord (chain), of gold, seeing:
  profit, remarkable improvement of your assets.
Coronation of a King or Queen, attending:
  prosperous success at present, favorable situation.
Corpse being buried:
  lovers soon to be separated.
Corpse, seeing:
  indicates a wedding.
Corpulence:
  increasing your wealth.
Corset (undergarment):
  vanity brings deep sorrow.
Cotton, waving:
  gain, profit.
Cotton shrub:
  riches, wealth.
Coughing:
  your secrets are being revealed.
Counterfeiting:
  shame, disgrace, misery.
Court, being prosecuted:
  confusion, perplexity.
Courthouse, standing in front of one:
  seeking your rights.

Courtroom:
  bad luck, repulsiveness.
Cover, seeking from enemies:
  fraud.
Cows, seeing:
  success in ventures.
Cow milk, drinking:
  unstable health.
Cow stable, being in it:
  relieved from an illness.
Cowl, seeing:
  peace of mind, state of bliss.
Crab, eating or seeing:
  declining business, pain, disagreement.
Cradle, seeing:
  bright future.
Crane (bird), seeing:
  bad omen, disaster, disloyal friends or servants.
Cranes (birds), flying:
  good news.
Cranes (birds) crying:
  joy.
Creditor, seeing or being visited by:
  secure, but effortless business.
Creek, with many fish:
  good inheritance.
Creek, with blood flowing:
  illness caused by blood vomiting.
Creek, dried out:
  poverty, lingering prolonging illness.
Creek, clear, seeing running into your house:
  means increase of fortune and wealth.

Creek, muddy, seeing running into your house:
illness, grief, sadness.

Creek, swelling, rising of water level:
growing assets, also fast declining of such.

Crescent, seeing:
secured food supply.

Crib, seeing empty:
bad paying work.

Crib, filled:
huge profit

Criminal (person), seeing:
disagreeable people.

Crippled person:
unexpected help.

Crocodile, seeing:
a warning about false people around you.

Crop (Goitre), on you, or seeing on others:
excessiveness makes you sick.

Crop (harvest), yellow without spikes:
your plans to succeed.

Crop (harvest), beautifully green:
big hopes for an upcoming acquisition.

Cross (holy), decorated with flowers:
happy family life.

Cross (holy), seeing:
sorrow.

Cross (holy), on your head:
defamation.

Crossbow, stretching:
fear and trouble.

Crossbow, breaking:
good future.

Crow (bird), crying:
receiving bad news.

Crow (birds), many on a tree:
a get-together of relatives.

Crow (bird), seeing:
indicates death.

Crown, seeing or wearing:
wealth and honour.

Crown of myrtle, seeing or wearing:
invitation to a wedding, or your own wedding.

Crowned, being:
sadness.

Cruelty, abuse:
you will be insulted.

Crust (scab), on the head:
acquisition of great wealth.

Crutches, using:
losing your lover, clumsiness in undertakings.

Crutches seeing, being used by others:
getting help, support from unknown friends.

Crying:
(see Weeping).

Cuckoo, seeing or crying:
joy and good health.

Cucumber, eating, or seeing:
illness.

Cuffs, on sleeves, wearing:
coming to honour.

Cuffs, on sleeves, of lace:
privilege.

Cuffs, on sleeves, dirty or with holes:
losing your job.

Cup (mug), breaking:
  death of an enemy.

Cup, made of silver:
  profit, gain.

Cup, letting it fall:
  nervousness, anxiety.

Cup, a nice painted one, breaking:
  imminent misfortune.

Cup (goblet), drinking from it:
  good times ahead, lots of fun at dinner party.

Cups (mugs), seeing:
  being surprised by an unexpected visitor.

Currant (red berry), eating or seeing:
  steadfast, perseverance.

Currant (white berry):
  satisfaction.

Currant (berry), seeing or eating:
  stability in love.

Currant (berry) black:
  unfaithfulness

Curl (ringlet):
  true love.

Curtain, seeing:
  discovering a secret.

Customs building:
  beware of cheaters.

Cypress tree, seeing:
  sadness, declining business.

Dagger, losing:
poverty.

Dagger, holding in your hands:
joy and honour.

Dagger, hitting a stranger:
luck in business.

Dagger, and bloodshed, seeing:
having secret sponsors.

Dagger, feeling danger to life:
swamped with charities.

Dagger, receiving from a dignitary:
great honour.

Dagger, seeing broken:
death, disease.

Dagger, seeing:
news from friends.

Dagger, pursuing a person:
victory over your enemies.

Dagger, being hurt by:
getting favors from friends.

Dairy, visiting:
being happy in your occupation, getting rich, or receiving honour, on trips happy times.

Dam, working on it:
good progress in your project.

Dancing:
unexpected good news from a distant friend.

Dancing and falling:
humiliation, arrogance.

Darkness, finding the way to the light:
rescue from great danger.

Darkness, being in it:
misery, difficulty.

Dates, giving away:
you will be kissed.

Dates, eating:
being favoured by a woman.

Daw, flying:
very bad news.

Dawn—rosy, seeing:
stormy days ahead.

Dead, seeing yourself:
lots of joy.

Dead, being and coming back to life again:
honour and happiness.

Dead, seeing a friend:
receiving news from an estranged friend.

Dead, people, seeing:
abused by friends, losing your lover,
losing on a horse deal.

Dead bodies, digging up:
experiencing cruelty.

Dead bodies, on a battlefield:
sorrow lies ahead.

Dead body with wreath, seeing:
lingering illness.

Dead person, seeing, eating with him/her:
great honour.

Dead people, seeing awakening:
dispute about inheritance.

Dead, being dead:
late marriage, luck in ventures.

Death—open casket:
unexpected inheritance.

Debt, paying off:
grief, worries.

Deer, seeing:
pursuing someone innocent.

Deer, seeing running:
means quick start in your trade

Deer, shooting:
inheritance, honour, humiliating weak and fearful enemies.

Deer herd, seeing:
many friendships.

Deer hind, seeing:
wealth, prosperity and happiness.

Dentist, seeing or talking to:
fraud and misfortune.

Denuding yourself, exposing to nudity:
experiencing shame.

Deprived, being:
losing a relative.

Desertion from your faith:
bad business deals, ruin.

Despair:
hardship, repulsiveness.

Devil, seeing:
bad luck, interruption in plans, tricked by false people.

Diadem, putting on:
losses, insults, offence.

Diamonds, seeing:
false luck.

Diamonds, receiving:
annoyance, bad luck.

Diamonds, eating:
happiness, reward, advantage.

Diarrhea, having:
indicates health.

Dice, seeing:
hostility, disagreeableness.

Dice, playing:
happy event, marrying chosen partner, wealth, honour.

Dinner, being invited:
you are well respected.

Dinner, smelling burnt:
unpleasant news.

Dirt, seeing:
damage through slander.

Dirty, being:
illness.

Dirty, making yourself:
happiness.

Dishes, of metal:
good marriage, or satisfaction.

Dishes, breaking:
brawl, dispute, feud.

Dishes, seeing:
domestic twist, disagreement.

Dispute, getting involved:
anxiety, fear.

Distill—cork, seeing:
annoyance, trouble.

Ditch, falling into:
caution about traps, falseness.

Ditch, jumping over:
treason, unfaithfulness.

Ditch, standing before a deep one:
means danger.

Doctor, seeing one who bandaged a relative:
impending marriage in the family.

Doctor, seeing with patient, having a friendly talk:
impending indisposition.

Doctor, visits you:
privilege and happiness.

Doctor, seeing:
for a sick person, health; for a healthy person, death.

Documents, receiving:
promotion.

Dog, white, seeing:
pleasant acquaintance.

Dog, being attacked by:
approaching danger.

Dogs being chased:
unsteadiness, excess.

Dogs, fighting:
family discord about inheritance.

Dog house:
decline in your social status.

Dogs, owning one yourself:
great wealth.

Dogs at play:
luck in business, reconciliation with those on bad terms, winning back estranged friends, truly being loved again.

Dolphin, playing:
misfortune or even death.

Domestic (servants):
lots of effort and work.

Donation, handing out:
piece of mind, satisfaction.

Donations, receiving:
change of luck.

Donkey, buying:
economy, gain.

Donkey, crying:
losses, damage and struggle.

Donkey, hitting:
being hard-hearted towards your loved ones.

Donkey, loaded with baggage:
Improving wealth, prosperous ventures, much respect.

Donkey, riding on:
slowly but surely reaching your goal.

Donkey, seeing:
in your love, loyalty and obligingness, prosperous business.

Door, burning or destroyed, seeing:
dying friends or relatives.

Dove, seeing:
pleasant news.

Dove, catching:
annoyance.

Dove cote:
peace and harmony.

Doves flying:
good news, luck in business.

Drag, seeing:
many obstacles in your ventures.

Dragon, flying:
false happiness.

Draw bridge:
unexpected trip.

Drawing (sketch):
truthful friends.

Dress closet:
luck and profit.

Dress fabric, seeing:
vanity causes heartbreak.

Dress, having a beautiful one:
coming into good circumstances.

Dress, stained:
sadness.

Dress, white:
luck in love and all ventures.

Dresses, black:
sorrow, losing your lover, painful experiences.

Dresses, blue or purple:
happiness, joy, prosperity, loyal friends.

Dresses, colorful, seeing:
*changing luck, annoyance by your lover, danger to lose
them, inconsistency in affections.*

Dresses, crimson:
old age, honour, your love was a happy choice.

Dresses, dark red:
*losing suspicious friends, quarrelling about pedantry,
annoyance from your children.*

Dresses, dirty, torn:
*difficulties in marrying the person you've chosen;
losing friends.*

Dresses, from other nations, seeing:
long trip ahead.

Dresses, green:
priority from your lover or suitor, or preferred offers.

Dresses, yellow:
falseness, jealousy, losing people who meant well.

Dresses, seeing or putting on:
luck, good circumstances.

Dresses, tearing apart:
   annoyance ahead, anger.
Dresses, washing:
   becoming economical, saving is recommended.
Dressing gown, wearing:
   indisposition experiencing.
Drink, given to you:
   invitation will be received.
Drink, mixing:
   imminent sickness in the family.
Drinking glasses, decorative:
   getting out of a bad situation.
Drinking fresh water:
   good omen.
Drinking from a glass:
   risk, revealing secrets.
Drinking vinegar:
   discord, dissension of family members.
Drinks:
   beware of your enemies.
Driving and turning over:
   forthcoming accident.
Driving, seeing:
   envy, jealousy.
Driving, in a car or carriage to a wedding or baby
christening:
   *to have honour and power, especially when a carriage is
   being pulled by people, and you don't get hurt.*
Drowning:
   prosperity and happiness.
Drowning, witnessing:
   triumph, victory over your enemies.

Drowned, being by someone else:
losses of all kinds.

Drum (drummer):
enduring small losses.

Drunk, being:
finding unexpected and unknown friends.

Drunk people, seeing:
repulsiveness, abhorrence.

Drunkenness, being addicted:
happiness and health.

Duck, beautiful, seeing:
great honour, for slanderous people it means losses and sorrow.

Ducks, catching:
success in receiving approval or acceptance.

Ducks, trying to catch:
casualties.

Ducks, swimming:
overcoming bad gossip.

Ducks, wild geese, flying:
joyful message.

Duel, participating in:
impending danger of death.

Dumb person, seeing:
charity brings blessings.

Dumplings, eating or making:
gossip will bring harm.

Dwarf (gnome):
being persuaded by weak enemies.

Dying:
receiving many empty promises.

Nostradamus' Egyptian Dream Interpretation Book

Eagle, your own:
strength in your intention.
Eagle, flying high in circles:
prosperity, wealth, honour, happiness in love.
Eagle, sitting on your head:
a death.
Eagle, standing or sitting on you:
for a rich person, death; for poor persons, goodness.
Earth, talking to:
very good, huge wealth and prosperity.
Earth, seeing split apart:
forthcoming danger.
Earthquake, feeling:
changes, uncertainty, unstable future.
Earth (soil), black:
annoyance, misfortune, affliction.
Earth (soil; ground), yellow or glowing:
happiness, success, loyal friendship
Earth (soil), being worked:
family growth.
Earthworms, seeing:
influential, powerful enemies.
Ears, beautiful or extremely large:
seeing a friend happy.
Ears, pulled:
unfair treatment, suppressed hopes.
Ears, like a donkey:
being abused.

Ears, cleaning:
loyal servants.

Earrings, wearing or seeing:
treason, effortless work.

Eating, seeing others:
an invitation.

Eating, yourself:
difficulties with your loved ones, misfortune in business, annoyance in love, arguments and trouble.

Eclipse:
losing many friends through defamation, getting a bad reputation.

Eel, removing from water:
for the sick, health; for the healthy, goodness.

Eel, seeing stripped down:
for a prisoner, freedom; for others, help from misery.

Eel, seeing dead:
sorrow and annoyance.

Eggs, belonging to you:
gain, harmony in the family.

Eggs, broken:
losses, arguments, poverty, separation from friends or lovers.

Eggs, eating:
becoming a father, happiness.

Eggs, dropping:
disharmony

Eggs, finding:
becoming a bride or groom.

Eggs, opening, rotten:
bad reputation.

Eggs, red, seeing:
anger, fire, death of a friend.

Eggs, seeing or buying:
good success in business, improving prosperity, promotion, good children, old age.

Eggs, seeing yellow:
serious illness.

Elder (bush):
recovery from an old, lingering health problem.

Elephant, seeing, being killed:
your plans are being destroyed.

Elephant, killed by you:
indicates death.

Elephant, seeing:
big plans, luck in business deals, late but good marriage.

Embroider (embroidery):
reaching for the unthinkable, being a slave in awe.

Emperor and kings, seeing:
lots of luck.

Endive, or other greens, eating:
difficulties.

Enemy, meeting:
overcoming unpleasantness, defeating rival, strengthening your position, overcoming all troubles.

Engagement:
growing family.

Engagement time:
reverence, veneration, worship.

Englishman, seeing or talking to:
false friends, bad creditors.

Entertainment (amusement):
losses.

Ermine, putting on, wearing:
happiness and great wealth.

Escape, helping:
because of your goodness, you earn inconvenience, trouble and difficulties.

Escaping:
avoiding danger.

Essences (perfume), using:
unfaithfulness, being cheated in general.

Estate, inheriting:
becoming a bride or groom.

Estate, buying:
return to being well-off.

Estate, selling:
decline in economic activity.

Estate owning, a beautiful one:
ability to have peace.

Estate, countryside, getting:
unexpected inheritance.

Estate, country, cultivating:
a lot of activity

Evergreen, seeing or picking:
loyal friendship.

Execution, witnessing:
dubious success in ventures.

Execution-place, going to or seeing:
happiness and honour.

Executioner, seeing:
forthcoming expulsion

Exile, being sent:
great love; for an ill person, health

Exile, received as a judgement:
changing views about business.

Eyebrows, falling out:
imminent disaster.

Eyebrows seeing, black:
  health.

Eyelids, big and beautiful:
  honour and respect.

Eyeglasses, your own, wearing:
  becoming vain, being laughed at, being fooled.

Eyeglasses, sunglasses, wearing:
  caution about friends.

Eyes, bad, weak:
  losses of all sorts, short on money.

Eyes, being robbed of them:
  *shattered hopes, losing a good friend,
  unpleasantness in love.*

Eyes, beautiful, your own:
  happiness and riches.

Eyes, good vision:
  you have good people around you.

Eyes, squinting:
  humiliating yourself.

Eyes, watering:
  bad future, losing your good reputation.

Fabric (garment), buying or seeing:
lucky projects.

Face, covering:
bad, serious news.

Face, refined in mirror, seeing:
your wishes being fulfilled.

Face, your own, beautiful:
proceedings in your projects and plans.

Face, your own, ugly, seeing:
many worries, sorrow.

Face, ugly, seeing in water:
enmity, hostility.

Face, beautiful, seeing in water:
long life.

Face, meeting a beautiful one:
much joy.

Face, pale:
illness, death.

Face, putting makeup on:
for a woman who doesn't need it, means good;
for a man, mockery and contempt.

Face, without a nose:
death.

Face washing:
remorse, repentance.

Factory (company), owning or seeing:
flourishing business.

Fair (market):
communication with many people.

Fainting:
unpleasant news.

Fairy, seeing or talking to:
much luck and happiness in all matters of life.

Falcon, golden:
great honour.

Falcon, flying:
being cheated.

Falling from a high place:
disaster, loss of honour and respect, and your fortune.

Falling, but holding on:
to be saved or protected from bad luck.

Falling over an obstacle:
getting information.

Falling and being hurt:
many conflicts.

Fan, hand held:
betrayal.

Farewell:
loyalty, friendship.

Farmer, seeing:
luck, happiness.

Farmyard:
rich inheritance.

Fat, eating:
illness.

Fat (stout) becoming:
means unexpected wealth.

Fat (oil), cooking:
indicates losses.

Fat, plump children, your own:
good years are ahead.

Father, becoming:
worrisome, but experiencing good times.

Father, of many children:
increasing worries.

Feast, attending:
unpleasantness, worries, discord in love, annoyance with children.

Feathers, being covered:
interruptions in business.

Feathers, black seeing:
recession in business, annoyance.

Feathers, taking:
indicates honour.

Feathers, white, owning:
being cleared from false suspicions.

Feather quill, writing:
good news.

Feathers, white, seeing:
welfare and amusement.

Feathers, seeing many flying:
hoping for luck, but in vain.

Feeding animals:
good progress in projects.

Feet, breaking:
receiving pity, because of an accident.

Feet, deformed:
ignorance.

Feet, dirty:
nasty sickness ahead.

Feet, seeing, not attached to a body:
imminent, soon danger.

Feet, sore:
finding support for your business.

Feet, washing:
falling ill, suffering.

Fence, seeing:
others want you in chains, handcuffs, to restrain you.

Festivities, attending:
painful news of sorrow.

Fever having:
unsteady love and friendship.

Fever, seeing others being affected:
happiness in marriage, peace of mind without wealth.

Field, green and beautiful:
*hope of good earnings, happy in love and marriage,
wealth and honour, in prospect of a prosperous position.*

Field, uncultivated:
stagnant plans.

Field, working over:
activity, keeping yourself busy.

Field, lay waste:
sadness.

Field, destroyed by hail:
false speculation

Field, in beautiful bloom:
success of your hopes.

Field, running through it, or on horseback:
soon receiving message from the person you await.

Field, planting and sowing:
*for those courting a woman and want children, good; for
others, work, illness and displeasure.*

Fig, eating or seeing:
happiness in marriage and love.

Fig, receiving as a gift:
friendly behaviour.

Fig tree, seeing:
being shielded, protected.

Fight:
(see Battle).

Fighting:
having a dispute, arguments.

Fighting on horseback:
getting a rich woman from a good family.

Fighting with wild animals and defeat:
being rescued from great danger.

Fighting-fencer:
frustration about your hopes, separation or loss of a lover.

Fighting and prize-winning:
happy ending in started ventures.

File (office), receiving:
warning or information about enemies.

Finding money or other things:
your worries will soon be lifted.

Fine, paying:
advantage.

Finger, burned:
falling into temptation.

Finger, cut and bleeding:
luck in love.

Finger, losing:
indicates harm or damage.

Finger, very nice, seeing:
respect and honour.

Fingernails, long and nice:
wealth, honour, a good wife, unexpected money.

Finger ring, losing or giving away:
suffering and lingering illness.

Finger ring, receiving:
great honour.

Fire (blaze), seeing:
unconditional love, wealth,
your children are being blessed.

Fire, blowing out:
abandon projects and plans.

Fire engine:
danger lies ahead.

Fire engines, driving fast:
imminent misfortune.

Fire, falling from sky:
experiencing hardship.

Fire, falling into:
great losses, ill humour.

Fire, bright flames, burning one or more buildings:
forthcoming honour, much goodness.

Fire, huge, seeing houses diminish in smoke and ashes:
disaster of all kinds, first in family members.

Fire, dropping:
bad omen.

Fire, seeing it go out on stove:
for sick a person, death.

Fire, small, on your stove:
riches, wealth.

Fire, running over it:
annoyance.

Fire, running away from it:
vexation ahead.

Fire, pail:
forthcoming danger.

Fire, burning bright:
being loved and not knowing it.

Fire, lighting, but not burning:
not being loved.

Fire signs, seeing in the sky:
rising cost of living, enemy invasion, a lot of misery.

Fireworks, seeing:
happiness

Fish, catching:
negligence

Fish, big, buying or seeing:
luck and advantage.

Fish, seeing:
bad profit, sadness, illness, annoyance.

Fish, eating, fried:
forthcoming prosperity.

Fish, seeing being sold:
unpleasant entertainment

Fish, small, buying or eating:
losses of all kind.

Fish, slippery, seeing:
a hope for profit diminishes, or unfaithfulness.

Fish, receiving as a gift:
bombarded with fake honours.

Fish pond:
avoid sloppiness and dirtiness.

Fishing gear, tackle, seeing:
fraud, persecution.

Flag, carrying:
you will be honoured.

Flag, flying in the wind:
danger, bad luck ahead.

Flames, clear and bright, seeing:
receiving money, or jewelry as a gift.

Flax, beautiful, seeing:
frugal in your household affairs.

Flax, spin to nice threats:
finding good accommodation.

Flattering, caress:
evil meaning.

Fleas, on you:
overcoming your enemies.

Fleas, seeing many, being bitten:
misfortune, poverty, difficulties.

Fleet, naval, full sails:
imminent changes.

Flies (insects), seeing many:
having enemies, being stalked, grief and insult.

Flies, killing:
hostility, overall eliminating of unpleasant things.

Flood, high tide, seeing:
*with people around you, or family members,
disagreements.*

Flood, seeing:
losses of all kinds.

Floor, in different patterns, seeing, or walking on:
great satisfaction through sorrow and joy.

Flour, seeing:
case of death.

Flour, roasting:
unexpected misfortune.

Flower bucket:
joy, instantaneous satisfaction.

Flowers, beautiful:
much joy.

Flowers, receiving as a gift:
honourable days.

Flowers, picking and binding together:
soon to be engaged.

Flowers, planting:
performing an act of kindness.

Flowers, scattered:
negligence, recklessness.

Flowers, tearing up:
someone is spoiling your happiness.

Flute, playing:
disagreements, losses.

Flying and falling:
inconvenience.

Flying, long distance:
pleasant days ahead, luck in ventures, praise.

Flying towards heaven:
for servants, good; for others, a trip; for the sick, death.

Flying, from a high perch:
arrogance.

Fog:
(see Mist).

Fools, seeing, or talking:
being cheated.

Foolish, being crazy:
remarkable success in business.

Foolishness, craziness by friends or loved ones:
reconciliation with enemy, attachment, great mentors.

Foot bridge, over water:
being frightened.

Foot path, narrow, walking:
don't leave the path of virtues, it is the only way to happiness

Forehead, high and wide:
indicates that you are using your head, concerns about decisions in your business.

Forehead, narrow and small:
you must show courage.

Forehead, wounded:
treason, finding out about it.

Forest, seeing:
a pleasant winter lies ahead.

Forest, seeing, walking through, logging:
happy marriage, peace of mind, receiving good fortune.

Forest, on fire:
enduring great losses.

Forest, walking in with great effort, endlessly:
defamation, pursuit, deceived by friends.

Forester's house:
being well-accepted on a trip.

Forest ranger, meeting:
imminent mischief.

Forge (iron), seeing:
getting plenty of work.

Forge, hammer, hearing:
you will hear something pleasant.

Forget-me-not, flowers:
you will be well remembered.

Fork, seeing:
being deceived.

Fortress, seeing:
unexpected opposition, hostility, also illness.

Fortress, (ruins) seeing:
sadness.

Fortress (ruins), climbing on:
fearless in any danger.

Fortress ruins, falling down from it:
being harmed.

Fortress, under fire:
war times.

Fountain, seeing:
a merry festivity ahead.

Fox, chasing or killing:
getting to know false friends and their tricky intentions.

Foxes, creeping, crawling:
secret enemies thinking of bringing you down.

French horn, musical instruments, seeing:
pleasant news.

Friend, seeing deceased:
unexpected novelty news, postponing marriage.

Friend seeing, welcoming:
to reach fame and honour.

Friends, insulting:
disdain.

Friends, joking around with:
separation.

Frighten, terrifying:
danger, bad luck.

Frills, ruffles, seeing:
vanity gets you in deep affliction or sorrow.

Frogs, seeing in pond:
plenty of money, lucky business, loyal love, married couple blessed with children, pleasant company on trips.

Frogs, catching or killing:
suicide, harming yourself.

Frogs, hearing them croak:
praise and fame.

Frostbite:
carefulness in all activities.

Fruit, giving away:
finding mentors and friends.

Fruit in baskets, seeing in storage:
good omen.

Fruit tree:
good continuation in your new business.

Fruit, seeing:
beware of opponents, forthcoming unpleasantness.

Fruit, sour, eating or seeing:
misfortune and illness.

Fruit, sweet, eating or seeing:
great fortune, happiness.

Frying pan, seeing:
harm, injury.

Frying spit, rotating:
bad luck and pursuit.

Funeral, arranging:
*for married couple, family additions; for single person,
impending marriage; for servants, promotion.*

Funeral, attending:
late marriage, mishap or death of a friend or relative.

Funeral, procession, seeing:
unexpected inheritance

Funnel:
don't reach for the unattainable.

Fur, receiving as a gift:
getting to know many mentors.

Fur, seeing:
progress in your occupation, trade.

Fur, wearing:
gaining respect.

Fury, bewitched people:
anger, rage, hate, enmity.

Gable, seeing collapse:
accident, death.

Gall-nut, oak apple, eating or finding:
culminate, slander.

Galley (slave):
courage, boldness.

Gallows, seeing:
false friends, misfortune, unrest.

Gallows, going to be hanged:
coming to honour.

Game of forfeits:
distraction is a disadvantage to your business.

Game (venison):
war, starvation, discord by lovers, dishonest friends.

Game (venison) meat eating:
prosperity.

Gamble (money):
quarrel, dispute.

Garden, neglected, disorganized:
being surrounded by false advisors.

Garden, beautiful landscaped, walking through:
*enjoying amusements, growth of investments,
forthcoming honour, good projects.*

Garden, high-fenced, seeing:
denial of requests.

Garlic smell:
repulsiveness, adversity.

Garment, buying:
happiness.

Nostradamus' Egyptian Dream Interpretation Book

Garter, wearing or seeing:
bad luck, annoyance.

Gate, seeing open:
your visitors are welcome.

Gauze, on hat or arm, wearing:
means sad, mournful message.

Gazebo with Jasmine flowers:
engagement.

Geese, seeing flying:
losses enduring..

Geese, seeing:
happiness, great wealth, absent friends seeing soon.

Geese, killing:
little pity for the needy.

Gem, seeing:
falling into temptation.

Gem, your own:
attain great honour.

Gem, receiving:
increasing your wealth.

Gem, wearing:
arrogance.

Ghost, seeing:
temptation to sin, danger, losing lover or friend, news of a death.

Giant, seeing:
good omen, success in business.

Gift, giving:
forthcoming new and honest friends.

Gift, receiving:
dealing with difficulties.

Gingerbread, eating:
pure joy.

Girl, seeing:
experiencing challenges.

Glass breaking:
disaster, fright, panic, death of loved relatives.

Glass, bursting while holding it:
separation.

Glass, cutting:
there is something to investigate, find out.

Glass, giving as a gift:
being well and fondly remembered.

Glass, seeing:
uncertainty in business, doubtful success.

Glide:
beware of allurement.

Globe, seeing or having:
going on a big trip, soon to be happily married.

Glory, well-deserved:
be careful of flatterers.

Gloves, having:
diminishing suspicion.

Gloves, seeing or putting on:
honour and happiness.

Glowing (fire), warming yourself:
quarrel with a friend.

Goat, billy goat, seeing jumping:
manipulating, playing tricks.

Goat, billy goat, being pushed by:
arguments ahead.

Goats, seeing:
comfort.

Goblet (cup), drinking from:
lots of fun at dinner party, good times ahead.

God, hearing him talk:
joyfulness.

God, praying to him:
great joy.

God, praising:
means suffering.

God, seeing or talking to him:
worries and grief.

God, worshipping or attending mass:
peace of mind, calmness.

God, worshipping, yourself celebrating mass:
hard and depressing work ahead.

Going astray:
many difficulties.

Gold bars, receiving:
unpleasantness, annoyance.

Gold (coins), seeing or getting:
being truly loved, soon to be married.

Goldfinch (bird):
interesting acquaintance.

Goldfish:
obstacles in business ventures.

Gold, giving as a present:
attending a wedding.

Gold, losing:
being robbed, or cheated in business.

Gold mine, discovering:
a sure gain, definite profit.

Gold, using as currency:
separation of friends, misfortune in ventures.

Gold, seeing or owning:
means flourishing success in started business.

Gold, stealing:
losing respect, or your lover.

Gold and silver dishes:
a flatterer is near you.

Gold, wearing:
fickleness, inconstancy.

Gooseberry, eating or seeing:
getting a grouchy husband or nagging wife.

Goose eggs:
having good nutrition.

Goose meat, eating:
lots of happiness.

Gorge (ravine), falling into:
bad omen.

Gospel:
receiving good advice and sympathy.

Gout pain:
forthcoming danger, experiencing unpleasantness.

Grain (corn), nice ones:
abundance, wealth.

Grain, cutting:
indicates joy.

Grain field, harvesting:
big earnings.

Grain field, seeing:
luck in love and ventures.

Grain, receiving:
joy, profit, gain.

Grain-spikes, wearing a wreath on your head:
honour.

Grain-spikes, picking:
flourishing business.

Grandchildren, your own:
everlasting well-being.

Grandparents, seeing or talking:
a good plan, carrying out.

Grapes, seeing:
blue: bad luck; white: joy; red: affliction

Grapes, bunches, cutting:
unexpected separation.

Grapes, getting as a present:
acquaintance.

Grass, seeing:
be alert about profiteers.

Grasshopper, seeing:
happiness is of a short duration.

Grass (cutting):
good times, wealth.

Grater:
being pursued by evil people.

Grave, climbing in:
false friends, defame, pursuit.

Grave, climbing out of it:
being lucky in ventures, receiving gifts, late marriage.

Grave, closing up with soil:
regaining your health.

Grave, preparing:
losing a friend.

Grave, seeing being prepared:
death of a relative.

Grave, someone is being carried out:
helping a friend, a friend becomes your beneficiary.

Grave, seeing:
discord, grief, postponed marriage.

Grave, with green grass:
hope and wishes coming true.

Gravedigger, seeing:
becoming sick.

Green peas, crunching and emptying them:
efforts in vain.

Greeted, being:
is bad.

Groom to be, or thinking you are:
disaster, loss of a friend or lover.

Grove, seeing:
going astray.

Grouse (white), flying:
unexpected news.

Guarantor, becoming:
for those ill, good; for those healthy, lots of expenses.

Guarantor, acceptance:
big disadvantage.

Guard, seeing:
be careful with whom you are acquainted.

Guests, accommodate:
friendship being returned.

Guests, bid farewell:
separation from a favoured thing.

Guests, welcoming:
soon to have visitors.

Guests, strange once, shelter:
unexpected happiness.

Guilty, being:
for a ill person, death; for a healthy one, a bad omen.

Guinea fowl:
saving, modesty, leads to a worry-free retirement.

Guitar, playing or hearing:
happy party.

Guns, seeing:
repulsiveness.

Gun powder:
being drawn to a dangerous gang

Gypsy:
beware of foolish tricks.

Hail, damage caused:
disaster and illness.

Hailstorm, seeing:
unpleasantness, annoyance, treason, wishes and hopes diminish.

Hair, being braiding:
connections will come about.

Hair curls, seeing:
becoming arrogant.

Hair combing:
luck in all business activities, dissolving disagreements.

Hair, entangled:
family quarrel.

Hair, grey having:
burdened with worries.

Hair, having red:
you have enemies.

Hair, losing:
going through bad times.

Hair, made up:
a jolly party lies ahead.

Hair, nice and black:
indicates health.

Hair, not wearing your own:
forthcoming illness

Hair, to have or see a braid:
old things are not always the best things.

Hair, seeing long:
being loved and respected.

Hair, cut off:
ease to worries.

Hair, to see it being cut off:
getting out of adverse matters.

Hairdresser, seeing or talking to:
experiencing distress.

Hall, bright, beautiful chandeliers and dancing in it:
great joy about a reconciliation.

Hall, beautifully furnished:
coming into your desired living standard.

Halberd, seeing:
bloody fight, bloodshed.

Ham, eating:
having many children, forthcoming wealth.

Ham, seeing:
reward and bonuses.

Hammer, seeing:
brutal treatment, hard labour.

Hammer, using to work with:
good progress in your work.

Hand, amputating:
disaster ahead.

Handbasket, holding:
worries about the future.

Handcuffed, being:
indicates cheating.

Handkerchief:
cleanliness is good for your health.

Hands, being wounded or dirty:
disadvantage, despise.

Hands, swollen:
being unsociable, quarrelsome.

Hands, washing:
to be honoured.

Hang, seeing a person:
receiving an honour.

Hanging, to witness one:
forthcoming illness.

Hanging, seeing yourself:
misfortune is imminent.

Hanging yourself, or being hanged:
fear and misery ahead.

Harbour, seeing:
delightful news, happiness and honour.

Harm, endure:
being honoured.

Harness, wearing:
rage leads to nastiness.

Harrow:
losses and illness.

Harp, seeing or playing:
disappointment.

Harpist, a female:
beware of reckless company

Harvest, a good one, being present:
your wishes soon to be come true.

Harvest, bringing home:
inheritance awaits you.

Harvesting in bad weather:
bad omen.

Hat, wearing, nice looking:
advantage, luck and recognition.

Hawk, seeing:
jealousy.

Hay, bad smelling, rotten:
disruption in business.

Hay wagon:
effort brings progress.

Hazelnuts, cracking:
obtaining good profit.

Head, another person's cut off:
good ventures ahead.

Head, amputated:
falseness and fraud from people around you.

Head band:
*occupying yourself with vanity, makeup and attire is
defacing you.*

Head, bald, seeing:
experiencing slander.

Head, extremely large, carrying:
triumph over your enemies, honour and dignity ahead.

Head of a coloured person, seeing or holding:
good news from distant friends or relatives.

Head, shaving:
dangerous, serious illness.

Head, washing:
avoiding a disaster.

Head, without body, seeing:
happiness and blessings.

Head with tangled hair:
twists and quarrel ahead.

Hearing loss:
carelessness.

Heart, bleeding:
offence, insult.

Heart, cutting up:
separation of a loving couple.

Heart, eating:
finding out when being assertive, love will be returned.

Heart, seeing:
tender loving.

Hedgehog, seeing:
your goodness is being used negatively.

Heel, injured:
bad luck of all kinds.

Hell, as described, seeing or being in it:
indicates changes of all kinds, suggested carefulness in ventures.

Hell, being rescued from:
peace, courtesies, support.

Hemp, tied together:
union is near.

Hemp, spin:
household activities.

Hen, big and nice, seeing:
happiness in loving.

Hen, hearing one cluck:
good and prosperous wedding, marriage.

Hen ladder, seeing:
effort leads to prosperity.

Hen, squealing:
disaster, annoyance.

Hen, seeing:
forthcoming insult, offence.

Hen, with chicks, seeing:
lots of children, grandchildren, overall, large family.

Herbs, eating:
long life.

Herbs, searching for:
mischief, gain.

Herd, seeing on prairie or meadows:
  prosperous future.
Herring, eating:
  avoid drinking parties.
Hermit, seeing:
  grief, worries.
Hip, having a big one:
  being blessed with descendants.
Hitting someone:
  you have to defend yourself.
Hole in your dress:
  carelessness.
Hole, crawling in:
  coming into hostile company.
Home, apartment:
  changes ahead.
Honey, eating:
  discomfort, misery.
Hood seeing:
  coming together, with a big fool.
Hop-culture:
  your ventures will prosper.
Horn twisting:
  getting out of sticky situations.
Hornet:
  news brings a lot of unrest and confusion.
Horns, having yourself:
  to be fooled.
Horns, from livestock, seeing:
  is not good at all.
Horseback rider, being thrown off:
  experiencing humiliation in your pride.

Horseback rider:
honour and dignity.

Horseback rider dismounting:
losing a friend.

Horseback rider, mount:
prosperity.

Horse, seeing bolt:
coming into danger of death through carelessness.

Horse, tumbling, or falling:
soon to encounter misfortune, bad luck.

Horse harness:
pleasant, worry-free life.

Horses, seeing or owning:
happiness, lots of joy.

Horses, seeing in front of a carriage:
soon to expect noble visitors.

Horses, thin, seeing:
losing your good reputation.

Horse stable:
effort and patience leads towards your goals.

Horse tail:
distinction, dignity.

Horse shoe, seeing:
soon to go on a trip.

Horse shoe, to see it being put on:
efforts and hard work.

Horse, being stubbed:
losing your lover.

Hospital:
coming into disgrace and shame.

House, being built:
luck in business and love, good and loyal servants.

House, being in it, and leaving:
gain, profit, advantage.

House, being demolished:
getting rid of an obstacle.

House, climbing up:
happiness, triumph, victory.

House, falling from, deep down:
careful in all deeds.

Household items, seeing a lot:
happiness in your marriage.

House, seeing burning, or collapsing:
disaster, unexpected case of death, losing your lover.

House, old, seeing:
long time friends, seeing again.

Hound:
bad business deals.

Hourglass, seeing:
a reminder that your lifespan on earth is limited.

Howling, hearing:
experiencing slander.

Human feces (stool), seeing:
great wealth

Human feces (stool), stepping into:
getting an unexpected large fortune.

Hungry, being:
*prosperity and honour are a result of diligence and
savings.*

Hunt:
through perseverance a happy future lies ahead.

Hunter:
a lot of effortless work.

Hunting, deers:
plans and projects are ruined.

Hunting, huge gems:
means great success in ventures.

Hurricane, violent:
losing your fortune.

Hut (cabin), seeing or being in it:
hard work.

Hyacinth:
receiving a gift.

Hymn, singing or hearing:
a festivity will soon take place.

Ice, seeing or gliding on:
near accident, pursuit, cheated in love, scattered hopes.

Ice, seeing in summer:
a useless beginning.

Icicles, hanging from your roof:
your love for each other grows deeper.

Island, seeing or being there:
abandoned by friends.

Illumination, seeing:
funny, joyful days ahead.

Imperfection, experiencing:
effort and work in vain.

Imprisonment:
comforting friends.

Infantry:
price hikes, bad times.

Infirmary, military hospital, being present at:
long-lasting illness.

Inheritance, receiving:
misery and grief.

Ink, seeing:
reconciliation with your enemy.

Ink, spilling over:
experiencing discord.

Ink pot, overturning:
hostility and repulsiveness.

Ink, writing with:
starting a new business.

Insane people,
  anger and revenge.

Inscription on graves, reading:
  loss of a family member.

Insects, seeing:
  losses, gossip, illness.

Instruments, musical, seeing:
  misadventure, death of a relative or acquaintance.

Intestines, seeing:
  joy and love.

Insulted, being ill-treated:
  annoyance and disagreement with household members.

Intoxicated, being:
  avoid excessiveness.

Invalid:
  caution, illness.

Itching (skin):
  you are going to make a mistake.

Iron (ironing):
  a lot of troublesome work.

Ivory, seeing:
  indicates poverty.

Nostradamus' Egyptian Dream Interpretation Book

Jail, being in:
   exaltation.
Jail, seeing:
   damage to your health.
Jaundice:
   great wealth, unexpected good fortune.
Jewish person, seeing or dealing with:
   betrayal, deception.
Jewish person, receiving service from:
   unexpected luck, advantage in all matters.
Jewelry, seeing or wearing:
   a nice gift awaits you.
Joy, experiencing:
   beware of foolishness
Joyful in your sleep:
   restlessness.
Jubilate (a shout with joy):
   disaster and sadness.
Judge, seeing or talking to:
   boring business.
Judgement:
   unpleasant news.
Judging, execution witnessing:
   false love, unfaithfulness.
Jug (pitcher):
   luck, joy, avoiding danger.
Juggler, seeing:
   beware of fraud.

Juice, handing to a sick person:
privilege.

Juice, squeezing:
worrying about the future.

Jumping into water:
danger, losing a friend or an acquaintance.

Jumping over a ditch, creek or fence:
overcoming imminent danger, avoiding a hostile plot.

Juniper:
evil gossip.

Kabal, playing:
  contempt.
Kettle:
  you are being well-accepted
Kettle (drum):
  big worries ahead.
Key, finding:
  being lucky in avoiding an embarrassment.
Key, losing:
  annoyance, dispute.
Key, using:
  being under suspicion.
Keychain-holder:
  family life brings lots of joy.
Killed, being yourself:
  fear and hardship.
King or queen, seeing or talking to:
  forthcoming honour, good business deals, achieving wealth.
Kissing a married person:
  bad omen of misfortune and disagreements.
Kissing a man, or seeing a man kissing:
  being unexpectedly deserted by friends.
Kissing nice girls:
  true and good friends.
Kissing somebody's hand:
  happiness and cheerfulness.
Kissing, wanting to:
  grief and depression.

Kitchen, cooking:
gossip.

Kitchen, seeing:
defamation

Knee, damaged seeing:
poverty, declining business.

Knee, laying on it:
humiliation.

Knee, swollen:
illness, exertion, losses.

Knife, with a nice handle:
receiving gifts, very soon.

Knife, seeing or holding:
persecution, disgrace, poverty, failing business.

Knight:
winning over a truthful friend.

Knitting:
diligence and perseverance make your plans succeed.

Knitted things, seeing:
bad omen, being fooled.

Knot, seeing:
embarrassment.

Knot, making:
causing others embarrassment.

Knot, undoing:
dissolving confusions

Labyrinth, seeing:
removal of all obstacles.

Labyrinth, walking through:
discovering secrets.

Laboratory:
serious illness.

Lackey (bellman):
unexpected great joy.

Ladder, seeing or using:
improvement of a situation, wealth and honour, happy marriage.

Ladder, placing:
being robbed.

Lady's maid:
laziness is dangerous.

Laying out, presenting:
good, for the poor.

Lamb, seeing hopping:
enjoying children.

Lamp:
giving out information.

Lamp, turning off:
destroying another's good prospects.

Lance, seeing or carrying:
disagreements, efforts in vain.

Landscape, scenery:
pleasant, fun trip.

Land, bare and deserted, seeing:
misfortune, annoyance, depression.

Land, beautiful, seeing:
getting a good wife.

Land, big and wide, seeing:
joy, amusement, fun, riches.

Land, strange and unknown:
loss of money, bad luck.

Land, prepared with lots of fruit, seeing:
good harvest, succeeding in ventures.

Lantern, burning:
secrets are being revealed

Lap, sitting on:
fondness.

Lard, seeing:
forthcoming difficulties.

Lark (bird), seeing:
rapid rise, success

Larkspur (flower):
being rescued from danger.

Last will (testament), drafting:
misfortune and dissatisfaction.

Last will (testament), seeing someone else's:
advantage and unexpected joy.

Lattice fence, facing:
liberation, inner peace

Laugh, hearing:
experiencing sudden joy.

Lavatory (toilet):
annoyance, boredom.

Law (claim), defending:
receiving recognition.

Lawyers, dealing with:
sorrow.

Lawsuit:
loyal friends.

Lawn, seeing or sitting on:
adventurous life.

Lead, being burned by:
falling into temptation.

Lead bullets, loading:
bad conscience.

Lead, melting:
hard working days ahead.

Lead, seeing:
wrongful prosecution.

Leaves, dry, withered:
interference in your plans.

Leaves, falling:
becoming dangerously ill.

Leaves, green, seeing:
experiencing pleasantness.

Learning (studying):
effort and endurance are overcoming all difficulties.

Leather:
complicated business ventures.

Leech, seeing:
self-interest, profiteering.

Lecture, giving or hearing:
your efforts are being rewarded.

Leg, artificial:
enduring bad changes.

Leg, having a swollen or ill one:
betrayal by friends, loss of a beloved one.

Leg, seeing being amputated:
losing a good friend.

Leg, seeing hurt:
misfortune.

Leg, strong, or seeing your own:
happiness, joy and success.

Lemon, eating or seeing:
happiness and peace of mind.

Lemon, squeezing:
being abused.

Lemonade, drinking:
invitation to a dinner party.

Lentil, eating:
annoyance and separation.

Lentil, dispersing:
harming yourself.

Lentil, seeing:
quarrel.

Lepers, keeping company with:
experiencing unpleasantness.

Lepers, seeing:
worries and struggle.

Leprosy, having:
promised great wealth, success in business.

Letter, receiving:
means forthcoming wealth.

Letter-case, seeing or finding:
resolving hidden matters.

Letters, burning:
irresponsible blows, tricks.

Letters, important, receiving:
means continuation in a good way, whatever you have started.

Letters, opening those addressed to others:
annoyance.

Letters, reading:
being trusted (enjoying).

Letters, sealing:
keeping secrets.

Letters, seeing, to be read:
request for caution

Letters, tearing, or torn, seeing:
ugly slander; giving up a good friend..

Letters, writing:
uncertain outlook.

Lettuce, eating:
good prospect.

Lettuce, sowing:
starting useless things.

Library, seeing or own:
finding good advice.

Lice, seeing or having:
receiving money.

Lice, killing:
avoiding an ugly persecution.

Life, losing your own:
unsuccessful business.

Light, bright, burning:
health and prosperity, soon an engagement.

Light, carrying, blown out by wind:
sudden death.

Light, faded, seeing:
joyful trip ahead.

Light of any kind, seeing extinguished:
forthcoming bad luck, losing a fight, disagreement.

Light or torch, extinguished, seeing:
sadness, sickness, poverty.

Lightening, seeing:
argument, disagreement, annoyance.

Lilies, seeing:
power and wealth.

Lilac tree:
illness and worries

Limb, losing a section of:
relief from something bad.

Limbs, deformed, seeing:
scare ahead.

Limousine, seeing:
pleasant future.

Limp:
your good reputation is in jeopardy.

Limp, seeing someone else:
ignorance enduring.

Linden tree:
fulfillment of your wishes.

Linen, fine quality:
enjoying happy days.

Linen, trading:
prosperous business.

Linnet, bird, seeing or hearing:
joy and good news from faraway relatives or friends.

Lion, seeing:
gaining wealth, respect from your superior, marrying a well-educated, rich lady.

Lion, locked up:
fear and difficulty.

Lion, killing:
overcoming your enemy.

Lions pursuing you:
being deserted.

Lion with cubs, seeing:
coming into danger.

Lips, beautiful, red, having or seeing:
prosperity and health of distant friends or relatives.

Liquor:
avoid flatterers.

Little, being:
exalt in your status

Liver, eating:
steady health.

Liver, cutting:
destroying your own health.

Liver, seeing:
having good, nutritious food.

Livery-Livree (official robe):
for servants, good; for masters, disadvantage

Livestock (herd), seeing:
prosperity.

Livestock, put to pasture:
disgrace, annoyance.

Lizard, seeing:
big chances in business.

Load, carrying:
fast, finishing business matters.

Loam (pit):
you are being followed.

Lock (pick), seeing:
being robbed.

Locksmith:
finding out a secret.

Locked up:
loss of happiness.

Logging (wood):
  a death.

Locomotive:
  beware, daydreamer (your head is in the clouds).

Lost, your belongings:
  judge your own opinion, and you will be well off.

Lottery draw:
  big losses.

Lotto, playing:
  cozy company.

Lover, seeing or being alone together:
  temptation.

Luck, having or sudden wealth:
  pursued by friends, harassed by creditors.

Lunar eclipse:
  losing your girlfriend.

Lute, playing:
  pleasant company

Lye, drinking or seeing:
  repulsiveness.

Lynx, seeing:
  discovering a person's cleverness.

Magic:
beware of swindlers.

Magnet, seeing or having:
experiencing popularity.

Magpie (bird), seeing:
to cheat.

Maid, girl, seeing:
happiness, and soon being united.

Makeup, using:
treason, falseness.

Malformation, deformity, seeing:
being hurt through slander.

Male nurse:
you are earning love and gratefulness.

Man, with nightcap:
too much comfort is not good for you.

Man (noble), elegant, seeing:
obnoxious people, surrounding you

Manure, seeing:
being dishonoured by bad company

Manure, loading:
servitude for a long time.

Manure wagon, driving:
unpleasant work.

Maple tree, seeing:
a comfortable life.

Maps, seeing:
a trip lies ahead.

Marble, seeing:
getting in and out of arguments.

Marder, killing:
freeing yourself of unpleasantness.

Marder, shooting:
good business with strangers.

Marketplace, seeing:
difficulty and hardship.

Marmot, seeing:
poverty and laziness.

Marriage-settlement:
sadness.

Masquerade, dressing:
prosperous business.

Masquerade, seeing:
being cheated.

Mass, attending:
inner peace.

Mass, celebrating by yourself:
getting difficult and depressing work.

Mask (face), seeing or wearing:
warning, hypocritical friends.

Matches, using or seeing:
riches, treasures.

Mattress, seeing:
restlessness.

Mattress, laying on it:
pleasant relations.

Matron, seeing:
reaching an old age.

Meadow, seeing:
you are going on a pleasant excursion.

Meal, having:
stinginess and poverty.

Meal, having with company:
abundance and riches.

Measles:
many hours of enjoyment.

Meat, feeding the dogs:
scornful treatment.

Meat, prepared, eating:
prosperity.

Meat, raw, bought by others:
arguments, disagreement.

Meat, raw, seeing or buying:
supportive friends, forthcoming wealth and honour.

Medal, seeing:
being neglected.

Medal (decoration), seeing or receiving:
coming into honour and reputation.

Medlar (tree with fruit like small apple), eating or seeing:
getting a good husband and having beautiful children.

Medicine, bitter taste:
repression from your enemies.

Medicine, to see being prescribed:
continuation of illness.

Medicine, handing others:
advantage and benefit.

Medicine, discharge through intestines:
good business deals.

Medicine (roots), seeing or eating:
end of annoying business.

Medicine, seeing:
indisposition.

Medicine, spitting out:
bad luck, trouble in your business transaction.

Medicine, taking:
repulsiveness.

Medicine, using:
loss of money.

Meeting a friend:
good omen.

Meeting an enemy:
bad omen.

Melons, seeing or eating:
unshakable love in marriage, an unsatisfying entertainer.

Merry-go-round, riding on or seeing:
coming into entanglements.

Merchandise, buying or selling:
activity in business brings huge profit.

Mercury:
unsteady, restless life.

Mermaid, seeing:
treason or prosecution.

Meteorological observation:
pursued by false friends.

Mice, seeing or catching:
successful business, good marriage and prosperity.

Mice, squeaking:
falling into grief.

Microscope, looking through:
try to improve your flaws.

Midwife, seeing or talking to:
happiness, publication of a secret.

Milk, drinking or eating:
advancing in your occupation, through economics.

Milk, buying:
success in many things.

Milk truck:
going on a nice trip.

Mill, seeing in operation:
happiness and riches.

Mill stone, seeing:
growing family.

Mill wheel, getting caught in:
coming into great danger.

Millet, eating:
a family life and big estate.

Milt (your organ), seeing:
festivities and fun.

Mine, seeing:
growth of wealth and property.

Miner (pitman), seeing:
unwanted visitor.

Mirror, breaking:
hostility.

Mirror, seeing:
for healthy people, joy and honour; for ill people, death.

Mirror, seeing yourself in:
being betrayed.

Mirror, with golden frame:
better status through extraordinary circumstances.

Miserable, feeling:
worrisome days.

Misery, great one, seeing:
contempt.

Mist (fog), covering the sun:
eye illness.

Mist (fog), disappearing:
being cleared of false accusations.

Mist (fog), dense:
encountering complex matters

Mite, maggot, seeing:
dispute at home.

Molasses:
using tricks to get you.

Mole, seeing:
injury, harm.

Monastery, seeing:
rest and peaceful old age.

Money, copper:
effortless work.

Money, counting:
happiness, great fortune.

Money exchange, stock trading:
lots of luck.

Money, finding:
profit, gain, good prospect for the future.

Money, full bags of:
secure, pleasant future.

Money, losing:
embarrassment, bad circumstances.

Money, metal, finding:
becoming happy.

Money, metal, paying with:
increasing respect.

Money, metal, receiving:
getting along well, joy.

Money, metal, seeing:
joyfulness, profit.

Money, paying with it:
freeing yourself from a burden.

Money, receiving:
nervousness, being restless

Money, seeing:
falling into temptation.

Money, wallet, full:
good progress in ventures.

Money, wallet, empty:
sustaining losses.

Monk, seeing:
being in good company.

Monks, talking to:
reconciliation, coming to terms with your offenders.

Monkey, killing:
overcome your enemy.

Monkey, seeing:
being cheated by flatterers.

Monkeys, seeing them bite (fleas):
illness; for people in love; their wishes will come true.

Monkeys, seeing dancing:
a lot of amusements and fun.

Monster, seeing:
much misfortune, annoyance, false hopes.

Monument, seeing:
sickness.

Moon, bright shining:
sincere joy, being truly loved.

Moon, seeing its first quarter:
succeeding in love and trade.

Moon, seeing through the water (reflection):
pleasant acquaintance.

Moon, seeing decline:
  fading love, damage in business trading.

Moor (land), dry, seeing:
  your hopes are being shattered.

Moor (land), green, seeing:
  indicates the last beam of hope.

Morgue, visiting or seeing:
  deadly peril, losing a friend.

Mortar:
  great festivity, pleasant visitors.

Moss:
  coming into much money.

Mosquito:
  bad company will bring you down.

Mother, seeing or talking to:
  seeing a long lost friend again.

Mountain, climbing:
  effort, unpleasantness.

Mountain, climbing, not reaching the top:
  declining ventures.

Mountain, collapsing:
  being trailed by a powerful enemy.

Mountain, descending:
  small but solid profit.

Mountains, seeing with green trees:
  great hope for the future.

Mountains, seeing with beautiful castles:
  shows steadfastness, firmness.

Mountains with ruins:
  interruption in your plans.

Mouse trap:
  beware of persecution.

Mouth, can't open:
deadly peril.

Mouth, huge:
mark of respect, enjoying good self-esteem.

Mouth organ, playing or seeing:
good news.

Mower, seeing at work:
luck and blessings in business.

Mower, seeing not in use:
losing friends.

Moveable goods, selling:
getting involved in lawsuits.

Muddy, dirty cloth, wearing:
misfortune and grief.

Mud, sludge, walking through:
difficult times ahead.

Muffs, wearing or seeing:
terrible times are coming.

Mule, seeing or riding:
being deceived and fooled by others.

Mulberry tree:
wealth and blessed years ahead.

Mulberries, eating or seeing:
late but happy marriage.

Murder, you being:
fright, shock experiencing.

Mushrooms:
falseness brings great drawbacks.

Mushrooms, eating or seeing:
reaching an old age.

Music, beautiful:
receiving good, merry news.

Mussels, seeing:
bad news from far away, embarrassment that takes great effort to eliminate.

Mustache:
idle, transient joy.

Mustard, coarse, eating or seeing:
bad omen.

Mustard, fine, seeing:
suffering from gossip.

Myrtle tree:
happily in love, enjoying respect, marrying a nice girl.

Myrtle, crown:
soon to be married.

Nails, finding:
luck, happiness.

Naked, yourself being:
ridicule and lots of sufferings.

Naked, seeing others:
luck and bright days ahead.

Navel, seeing:
increasing your wealth.

Neck, big and thick:
happiness.

Neck, small and thin:
misfortune.

Neck (throat), being choked by a person:
that same person will influence you.

Neck (throat), seeing:
good omen.

Neck (throat), swollen:
happiness.

Necklace, neck ribbon, seeing:
honour and happiness.

Necklace, wearing:
to be privileged, honoured.

Necktie, seeing:
for the not-so-fortunate, a good omen; for the fortunate, losses or imprisonment.

Necktie, taking off:
being protected against a cold.

Needful, being in need:
forthcoming bad luck.

Needles, seeing or using:
arguments.

Negro, seeing:
disaster in undertakings.

Neighbour, seeing or talking to:
coming into danger.

Nets, seeing:
corruption will bring harm.

Nettle:
libel, pursuit.

Nest, empty, seeing:
happy marriage.

Nest, full, seeing:
additions to the family.

Night birds, seeing:
never start anything before thinking it over twice.

Nightingale, seeing or hearing sing:
joyful news in your engagement time, happy marriage.

Night owl, flying:
chaos between your loved ones.

Night owl, on top of house, and crying:
a bad omen.

Night watchman:
thieves, causing harm.

Nose, big, your own:
obtaining wealth and honour.

Nose, bleeding:
enduring ignorance.

Nose, short:
modest circumstances, but happy, peaceful family life.

Nose, clogged:
an influential man is leaving you,
deceitful loyalty and friendship.

Noise, turmoil:
nervousness and restlessness in the house.

Northern lights, seeing:
your nicest dreams and hopes come true.

Notary, consulting:
soon to be married.

Notary, seeing him/her write:
being mentioned in an inheritance.

Numbers, seeing:
through stupidity, you will lose a lot.

Numbers, picking those you favour in a draw:
good prospect of big earnings.

Numbers, writing:
a lot of activity and things to do.

Numbers, seeing:
under 90, uncertainty; over 90, luck and prosperity.

Numbers, seeing and not remembering:
merry, fun social gathering.

Numbness, freeze:
work in vain.

Nun, seeing or talking to:
entering a different social status.

Nuts, eating or seeing:
wealth, happiness and honour.

Nuts, playing with:
arguments.

Nuts, walnuts, seeing:
annoyance and misfortune.

Oak tree, beautiful, seeing:
advantage, wealth, long life.

Oak tree, dried out:
death of a relative or friend.

Oath, to take or see being taken:
involvement in lawsuits.

Obelisk, seeing:
surprised through extraordinary events.

Ocean, or big sea, crossing:
disaster.

Ocean:
(see, "sea")

Ocean birds, seeing:
for travelers on sea, danger.

Offence, being offended:
favour and kindness.

Office, being there:
great losses, your debtor lets you down.

Oil, beating with mixer:
contestation.

Oil, burning:
much effort in vain.

Oil, being poured over you:
advantage.

Oil, tasting (a good one):
strong health.

Oil, seeing spilled:
tremendous losses.

Oil, saving, scooping up:
luck and advantage.

Ointment, making:
illness.

Old, being:
liberty, freedom.

Old, becoming:
evil, bad.

Olives:
fond of sweetness, hasty behaviour.

Onions, cooking:
coming into needs, being bothered by authorities.

Onion, eating:
mourning.

Onions, seeing:
secrets are being revealed.

Opera glass, seeing:
news awaiting.

Opponent, meeting with him:
misfortune.

Oranges, eating or seeing:
suffering from lingering indisposition.

Oranges, bitter tasting:
loss of honour and wealth, being misjudged.

Orchard, walking through:
becoming rich because of inheritance, happy marriage, many good children, true love, influential friends.

Organ, seeing or hearing being played:
joy or inheritance.

Ornament (jewelry), seeing:
vanity creates heartbreak.

Ostrich:
making a fuss about nothing.

Otter, fish, catching:
  luck in business.

Overcoat:
  seeing great dignitaries.

Owls, crying:
  vexation, annoyance.

Owls, seeing:
  discontentedness, illness, poverty.

Ox, seeing at work:
  servitude, bondage.

Ox, seeing:
  advantage in trade affairs.

Ox, seeing jumping:
  coming into danger.

Oysters, eating or seeing:
  success in your work, happy pregnancy.

Pail or water bucket, seeing:
comfort.

Pain, feeling:
hardship, luckily overcoming trouble.

Painting, seeing a portrait of yourself:
long life.

Painting something white:
pursuit, persecution.

Painting something black:
illness.

Painting something in red:
joy.

Painting, seeing:
being tempted by false friends, danger, deceived by lover, loss of a friend

Palace:
arrogance brings you down.

Palisade, conquering or destroying:
security, glory, happiness.

Palisade, seeing:
embarrassment and restlessness.

Palm, branches, seeing, carrying or collecting:
abundance, wealth, luck in business.

Panther, seeing:
being frightened.

Pantry, seeing:
sickness and bad luck.

Paper, cutting:
worries about the future.

Paper, printed, seeing:
inspiring trust.

Paper, tearing apart:
coming into anger.

Paper, writing on:
suing and defamation.

Parade, seeing:
the thirst for pleasure brings big disadvantage.

Paradise, being in:
being remember and identified with a lovely item.

Paralyzed, being:
misery, hardship.

Parcel, carrier:
effort and work keeps a healthy spirit.

Parchment:
unexpected inheritance brings joy.

Parents, arguing with them:
bad omen.

Parents, seeing or talking to:
good fortune in ventures, cheerfulness.

Parents, siblings, seeing deceased:
confusion, bad luck.

Park, seeing:
a comfortable life.

Parrot, seeing:
coming to know of secrets.

Parrot, talking:
disgusting gossip.

Party, attending a social gathering:
danger of one's life.

Partridge, seeing:
lustful desires.

Pass (mountain):
hard, troublesome work.

Passport:
going on a big trip.

Pasture (land), seeing:
danger and difficulty.

Path, walking on a wide one:
happiness.

Path, walking on a narrow one:
grief and annoyance.

Pavement, seeing:
bad omen in every way.

Pawn shop:
recklessness leads to losses.

Pawn shop, entering:
bad business.

Peaches, breaking in half:
coming into your desired lifestyle.

Peaches, seeing or eating:
reunion with your estranged lover.

Peacock, seeing:
rapid progress in ventures, many lucky connections, many courtesies on a trip.

Pearl, seeing or owning:
misfortune, discomfort.

Pearls, sorting:
lonely, boring life.

Pear tree, shaking:
intemperance.

Pears, beautiful looking, hanging on a tree:
good prospect for the future.

Pears, being eaten by insects:
insidiousness.

Pears, good ones, seeing or eating:
overcoming disagreements.

Pears, sour, eating or seeing:
annoyance in your household.

Peas, eating:
luck in ventures.

Peas, planting:
hopes in succeeding of your plans.

Peas, seeing or picking:
prosperity, growing wealth, cheerfulness.

Peas, nice, growing and blooming:
good progress in your deeds.

Pencils:
receiving a good message.

Penitentiary:
rescue from imminent danger.

Pennant, seeing:
people of authority favour you.

Penny, seeing:
charity brings reward.

People, coming towards you:
sadness, affliction.

People, dressed in black:
coming into danger of death.

People, seeing many:
bad luck, disaster.

People, old, seeing:
good luck.

People, old, honouring:
lots of blessings.

Pepper, seeing or using:
being offended.

Pursuing:
unpleasantness.

Petrel (storm-birds):
risky wanderings.

Petticoat, colourful, seeing:
doubtful success in love or otherwise in business.

Petticoat, white, seeing:
a rare enjoyment.

Pharmacy, seeing, being in it:
meeting with profiteers and evil people.

Piano, playing or seeing:
dispute, conflict between friends.

Pictures, beautiful, seeing:
being cheated.

Pictures, seeing big and bad looking ones:
finding friends, being happy.

Pies, pastries:
excess leads to illness.

Pigs, seeing:
deceived by servants, remove unpleasantness.

Pig, rolling in the mud:
getting a evil housekeeper.

Pig shed:
disadvantaged business.

Pike seeing:
coming into danger.

Pills—tablets, seeing:
beware of folly and fools.

Pilgrim seeing:
news from abroad.

Pilgrimage:
your start is commendable.

Pillar seeing:
honour.

Pillar collapsing:
invalidism, illness.

Pin-cushion (needles):
a nice gift will surprise you.

Pin, seeing or having:
getting lots of rewarding work.

Pineapple eating:
being invited as a guest.

Pipe, seeing:
pleasant circumstances.

Pistol:
pursuit by enemies.

Pit, seeing or falling into:
sudden misfortune, being tricked.

Pit, climbing out with great effort:
pursuit, having friends unknown to yourself.

Pit, getting out with ease:
overcoming many big difficulties.

Pith (stone) collecting:
a long lasting plan becomes reality.

Place, seeing:
friendly reception.

Plains, seeing:
happiness and enjoyment.

Planting:
prosperity and authority, prestige.

Plaster-ornaments:
disaster in your plans.

Plaster (white wash):
huge expenses are ahead.

Pliers, seeing or having:
treason or pursuit.

Plow, seeing, or your own:
soon to be happily married.

Plow, destroying:
interruption in your trade, job.

Plowing:
good progress in business.

Plums, eating or seeing:
bad times ahead.

Plums (Italian), oval, freestone, eating:
shock, sickness.

Plums (Italian), freestone, hanging on trees:
prosperous future.

Poison, giving somebody:
disagreement, annoyance.

Poison, taking and dying:
giving bad advice.

Polecat:
miserable illness.

Poles, sticks:
disagreements.

Police:
repulsiveness, disagreements ahead.

Pomegranates, seeing:
coming to wealth through a last will or luck.

Pond, seeing a little one:
*getting a beautiful woman, wishes come true, joy from
your family.*

Pope, seeing or talking to:
happiness, cheerfulness.

Poplar, whisper or seeing:
a good outcome from a project.

Poppy seed head, seeing:
becoming ill.

Porcupine:
warning about mockery and envy.

Pork meat:
remain in an ordinary social class.

Portraying yourself:
long life.

Portraying, by a painter:
having good friends.

Portrait, seeing:
long life for the person you have seen.

Portrait, your own, giving away:
treason, betrayal and disagreements.

Portrait, a beautiful girl:
soon to be married.

Portrait, carrying and breaking:
imminent disaster.

Portrait, seeing it being painted:
abide in your love.

Portrait, receiving as a gift:
lots of fun ahead.

Post (stake), pushing into the ground:
effortless work.

Post (delivery) wagon:
pleasant news.

Potatoes, digging:
effort, getting little thanks for hard work.

Potatoes, eating or seeing:
becoming ill.

Pots, seeing:
gaining wealth.

Pots, breaking:
a fun party.

Poultry, feeding:
soon to be engaged.

Praying:
joy and peace of mind.

Prayer book:
comfort in sorrow.

Preaching:
moderate lifestyle keeps your health and well being.

Pregnant woman:
unpleasantness lies ahead.

Pregnant woman, making fun of:
being freed of worries.

Priest, standing in pulpit:
experiencing repulsiveness.

Prison, being released:
illness, death.

Prison building, seeing:
inner peace.

Prison, being escorted into:
happiness and well-being.

Prison, living in it:
comforted by friends.

Procession, attending or seeing:
happiness and joy.

Profit, receiving:
arrival of a friend.

Profiteer, talking or doing business with:
illegal business temptation.

Profiteering:
shame, loss of fortune.

Property, estate, beautiful and large inheritance, receiving as a gift:
happy and profitable marriage.

Prostitute, seeing or talking to:
happy days and luck.

Protection, finding:
misery, ramification.

Protractor, seeing:
you will commence construction.

Provoke:
hostility, discord.

Pub (inn) lodging:
staying calm during disagreements and complaints.

Pub (saloon), seeing:
getting rest.

Public festival, attending:
unstable luck, personal mishap.

Puddle:
corrupt company gives you a bad reputation.

Pulpit, standing in it, or seeing:
being honoured in public.

Pump in action:
surprises, very good omen.

Pump (well), empty or dry:
poverty, misfortune, bad luck.

Pumpkin, eating:
sickness.

Pumpkin, playing with:
separation from a favoured thing.

Pumpkins, seeing hanging:
having many mentors.

Puppet show, seeing:
getting a subordinate job.

Puppet:
loyal, devoted servants.

Purchasing, something:
extravagance, waste, brings disadvantage.

Purgatory:
be careful not to sin.

Purse, wallet, an empty one:
sustaining losses.

Purse, wallet with money:
good advancing business transactions.

Pyramids climbing:
good business.

Pyramids seeing:
happiness and honour.

Quail-bird, seeing or hearing:
dispute, treason, disagreement, bad luck in marriage.

Quarrel:
unexpected news.

Quackery:
stupidity brings harm.

Quince (fruit), seeing:
happiness in marriage, wealth, peace of mind.

Rabbi:
soon to be in pleasant company.

Rabbit meat, eating:
peace of mind.

Rabbit, seeing:
fear, fearing death.

Rabbit, shooting:
being happy.

Radish:
simple nutrition keeps you healthy.

Rage, getting into:
a long overdue business matter comes to an end.

Rain, downpour, seeing:
efforts in vain.

Rain, downpour, going into:
losing courage and balance.

Rain, being in it:
happiness in the family, constant love.

Rain, thunder and lightening, getting wet:
trouble ahead and bad luck.

Rainbow, seeing:
lots of efforts in vain, troublesome luck.

Raisins:
excessiveness brings ruin.

Rake, seeing:
expect some news.

Ram, being kicked or pushed by:
pursuit.

Ram, seeing:
  profit.

Ranger, meeting:
  imminent mischief, unpleasantness.

Raped, being:
  disaster in every way.

Raped, in public:
  disaster and declining enterprises or ventures.

Rasp:
  a lot of uproar for nothing.

Raspberries, eating or seeing:
  enjoyment and pleasure are awaiting you.

Rats, catching:
  settling a dispute.

Rats, seeing:
  many enemies, deceived by friends.

Ravens claws, seeing:
  disaster and disagreements.

Raven, flying around you:
  death.

Reading:
  you will get good news.

Reaper:
  luck in business.

Receipt:
  losses ahead.

Reed (plant), seeing in water:
  indecision brings drawbacks and disadvantage.

Relatives, seeing or talking:
  delusion, fraud.

Relic, seeing:
  danger of losing money and estate.

Resting, relaxing:
danger ahead.

Respect, showing:
humiliation.

Respect, receiving:
favourable establishments.

Restaurant, inn:
great unrest lies ahead.

Restaurant, serving meals:
creating hatred and envy.

Resurrection of the dead:
rescue from misery.

Retailing (selling):
treason, pursuit.

Revenge:
long-lasting involvement in a lawsuit.

Review of troops:
imprisonment.

Rib, seeing:
happiness in the family, luck in business.

Rice, eating or seeing:
plenty of money and assets are forthcoming.

Rich, being:
in danger of losing everything.

Rich (wealthy) people, seeing, talking to
or being friends with:
receiving comfort, rewards and good deeds.

Rifle, going hunting:
unfaithfulness.

Rifle, seeing a nice looking one:
falling in love.

Rifle, shooting one:
big embarrassment.

Ring, hammering around a barrel:
new connections.

Ring of gold and precious stones:
coming into well-off circumstances.

Ring, finding:
happiness lies ahead.

Ring, giving as a present:
becoming a bride or groom.

Ring, losing:
unexpected separation from a lover, friends or relatives.

Rivalry:
unsuccessful ventures.

River, crossing over:
overcome dangerous enemies.

River, crashing over rocks:
a family member faces ruin.

River, falling into:
misfortune.

River, overflowing:
stop, project is being hindered.

River, being swept downstream:
annoyance, danger, persecution.

River, roaring:
slander, blasphemy.

Roaring, howling of animals:
bad news.

Roast beef, eating or seeing:
profitable, good business.

Roast, smelling:
running unnecessary errands.

Robber, being slayed by:
losing inheritance.

Robber, seeing or being held up by:
casual ties with relatives, children or fortunes.

Rock, ascending easily:
reaching your goals.

Rock climbing:
conquest.

Rock, climbing and not reaching the top:
a stand still, decline in business.

Rock, descending from easily:
losing friends or relatives.

Rock, tall, seeing:
dealings with an enormous project.

Rock, seeing:
work and effort.

Rocket, seeing rising:
changeable luck, unsteady in love, invitation to a happy party.

Rod, someone hitting:
advantage, overpowering.

Royalty, on horseback or in a carriage:
leaning towards wastefulness.

Royalty, seeing:
honour.

Royalty, talking to:
being envied.

Roof, full of swallows:
going on a trip.

Roof, eaves, standing under:
unpleasantness, difficulty.

Roof, falling down from:
unpleasant news.

Roof, seeing on a house:
domesticity, family life.

Room, sweeping:
effort and tenacity leads to your goals.

Rooms, nicely wallpapered:
flourishing trade.

Rope, being made:
means declining prosperity.

Rope, being tied up:
good fortune and honour.

Rope, cutting:
harming others.

Rope, climbing down on it:
danger in your activities.

Rope (tight rope) walker:
a risky venture brings harm.

Rooster, crowing:
caution.

Rooster, seeing:
being liked by women.

Roosters fighting:
difficulty in marriage.

Rosebuds:
discovery of a precious object.

Rosebush with many roses:
family additions.

Roses, seeing faded:
vexation, unsteady love, bad luck.

Roses, in full bloom:
happiness and blessings.

Rosemary, seeing:
you will earn a good reputation.

Rosehip, eating:
poverty.

Roots:
secure living standard, being well-off.

Rowing:
having hard, but rewarding work.

Ruins, seeing:
being sloppy brings harm.

Rum, drinking:
excessiveness damages health.

Running, and not moving ahead:
much effort in vain.

Running, or seeing someone run:
fulfillment of your wishes, being lucky.

Sabre:
   perseverance brings you towards your goal.
Sack, bag, heavy, carrying:
   harmful times.
Sacks, full, seeing:
   abundance in all earthly things.
Sack, being carried:
   lots of expenses.
Sack, seeing with holes:
   losses.
Sacks, many piled on a wagon:
   flourishing trade.
Sad, being:
   making friends.
Sad, being, not knowing why:
   very bad omen.
Sailor, seeing or talking to:
   misfortune on trips.
Sailor, arriving on a ship:
   news from a friend or relative who lives far away.
Sailboat:
   a big trip ahead.
Saint, worship:
   blessed at your work.
Salad:
   a time of tests lies ahead.
Saliva and vomiting:
   excess ruins your health.

Salmon, eating:
  you will have a discovery.

Salt, scattering:
  annoyance.

Sand, seeing:
  insecurity in everything.

Sausage, eating:
  unexpected visitor, flirtation.

Sausage, seeing or making:
  struggle.

Saw, seeing your own:
  a business deal is happily finalized.

Saw, seeing or using:
  good progress in your business.

Scabs (itch), having:
  unnecessary fear and worries.

Scaffold, seeing:
  be on guard.

Scale, seeing:
  you will make good business deals.

Scandal:
  disagreements, hostility.

Scared, being:
  grief and shortages of food.

Scarecrow:
  having dishonest friends.

Scars, getting or having:
  honour and glory.

Scepter:
  demanding behaviour is disliked.

School, attending:
  happiness.

School or school children, seeing:
being cheated, sorrow.

School teacher:
difficult and troublesome business.

Scissors, using:
involvement in something unpleasant.

Scissors, seeing:
gain, profit.

Scorpion, seeing:
be careful, malicious enemies.

Scuffle, fight:
don't get involved in the affairs of others.

Scythe, to own or see:
being offended by friends.

Scythe, mowing or seeing:
shows gain, profit, getting hard working servants.

Sea, calm and cruising:
happy union, coming into great riches.

Sea, cruising, landing on a deserted place:
with effort and difficulty you will reach your goal at last, reward through success.

Sea, stormy and cruising:
lots of complaints in love or business.

Seal, seeing:
joyfulness.

Seal (signet ring) using:
coming out of threatening danger, enjoying security.

Sealing (letters):
many business deals.

Seats (stools), seeing:
distinction, honour.

Secluded (place), being there:
illness and danger.

Seeds, picked by birds:
losing confidence.

Seed, selling:
flourishing business.

Seeds, sorting:
means good progress in business.

Seeing your deceased relatives and friends:
grief and sorrow.

Seminar, attending:
betrayal, or being fooled.

Sentenced, seeing people:
losing some of your friends.

Sentry box, seeing:
being safe from enemies.

Seraglio (harem):
exuberance is the ruin of the soul and body.

Sewing kit:
increases in your income.

Sewing, stitching:
your work comes in very handy.

Shadow, walking in it:
withdrawing from an oppressing relationship.

Sheaf, tying together:
new acquaintance.

Sheaf, loading, harvesting:
efforts are being rewarded.

Sheafs, seeing:
humiliation from your enemies.

Sheafs, lots of spikes, seeing:
good fortune.

Sheep, grazing:
health and happiness.

Sheep, pushing each other:
suffering.

Shepherd, seeing:
caution in ventures.

Shepherd, seeing with a herd:
gaining wealth.

Shelter from rain:
hidden annoyance.

Shelter, seeking from enemies:
fraud.

Ship, building:
grandiose, giant projects.

Ship, burning:
huge losses.

Ship, fighting the waves:
lots of conflict with your enemies.

Ship, in harbour:
no change in your tasks.

Ship, machinery, seeing:
unexpected news from your creditors.

Ship, sailing under a bridge:
approaching danger, and luckily overcoming it.

Ship, seeing or being on it:
unexpected good news.

Ship, sinking:
frightened by sad news.

Ship, stranded:
big embarrassment.

Ship, with many passengers:
emigration.

Ship, without sail or mast:
rescue from trouble or misery.

Shirt, taking off:
frustrated hope.

Shirt, torn, seeing:
means great success.

Shirt, seeing:
forthcoming prosperity.

Shirt, washing or ironing, seeing:
striving for affection.

Shock (terror):
joyful news.

Shoes, buying:
overly hasty.

Shoes, cutting apart:
getting sore feet.

Shoe, fitting:
for your business, suitable undertakings.

Shoe, new, trying on:
good omen.

Shoe, sole, losing:
trouble, inconvenience ahead.

Shoe, too tight, putting on:
severe depression.

Shoemaker, seeing:
troublesome life.

Shooting:
through endurance, reaching your goals.

Shopping:
advantage, gain.

Shore, going for a walk:
getting into danger.

Shot, hearing:
complications.

Shotgun, shooting:
anger, false hopes of profit.

Shoulder, broken:
unpleasantness.

Shoulder, deformed:
loving other women.

Shoulders, shrug:
having doubt in your plans.

Shoulders, extremely high:
strength and patience.

Shoulders, swollen:
annoyance with your loved ones.

Shovel, seeing or using:
getting unrewarding work.

Shroud, seeing:
long-lasting illness.

Shrub (bush), seeing:
falling in love quickly.

Shrub or bushes, cutting down:
seeing unpleasantness diminish.

Shrub or bushes, hurting you:
losses in business.

Shrub or bushes, walking through quite some distance:
obstacles of different kinds.

Siblings, seeing deceased:
long life.

Siblings, seeing dying:
losing enemies.

Sick, and being in pain:
misery and bad luck.

Sickness, suffering from a hidden one:
dishonourable wealth.

Sick people, visiting and comforting:
joy, cheerfulness, happiness.

Sickle, seeing or using:
profit.

Sickle, sharpening:
pleasant messages.

Side of your body, being swollen or injured:
great wealth and happiness.

Sieve, seeing:
an unanswered request.

Sign, seeing:
involvement in disputes.

Sign, plate of an inn:
beware of rivalry.

Sign post:
coming into a tricky situation.

Silk dress, wearing:
entering desired status in society.

Silk dress, tearing:
not knowing a good thing when it's offered to you.

Silk, red colour, seeing:
forthcoming casualty.

Silk, seeing or using:
flourishing business.

Silkworm, finding or seeing:
many truthful friends.

Silk material, woven:
hesitation in your course of business.

Silver, seeing:
pursuit by false friends, deceived by your lover.

Silver, dishes:
coming into good circumstances.

Silver, small coins, seeing:
unpleasantness, losses.

Silver, precious metals, seeing or receiving:
joy, money and possessions.

Silver things, wearing:
servitude.

Silver pieces, your own:
difficulty.

Silver pieces, selling off:
improvement in business.

Single, being:
union.

Singing:
you will hear uncomfortable things.

Singing, hearing:
good news will come from far distant friends or relatives.

Singing in the bathtub:
losing your voice.

Singing in front of a sovereign:
becoming critical and fault finding.

Singing, nice songs with a clear voice:
everyone is well and happy.

Singing with a fun crowd:
getting opinions from many different people.

Siskin (bird), seeing or hearing:
be steadfast in your plans.

Sisters or brothers, seeing or talking to:
annoyance, disagreements.

Skating:
means much success.

Skating, seeing:
interruptions in your business.

Skeleton, seeing:
shock, being frightened.

Skeleton, animal, seeing:
arguments, quarrel about pedantry.

Skeleton bones, seeing:
trouble and unpleasantness.

Skin, eczema:
careful, danger to your health.

Skin, dark coloured or black, seeing or your own:
being cheated by friends or relatives and left behind.

Skirt, too tight, wearing:
experiencing hardship.

Skirt, full of spots:
defamation, slander.

Skull (cross-bones), seeing:
finding out about hidden secrets.

Sky, clear, blue, sunny, seeing:
lots of joy, being lucky in ventures, your partner takes you to the altar.

Sky, cloudy, red or dark, seeing:
vexation, feud, annoyance with your superior.

Sky, flying up to:
modest wishes are being granted.

Sky, lots of clouds:
unfaithfulness.

Sky, seeing the sun:
discovering clarity in a twisted matter.

Slap in the face:
keeping evil company.

Slapping someone:
peace and calmness in your family, good progress in your approach to love.

Slate:
effort completes your task.

Slaughterhouse, seeing, or being in:
fatal projects.

Slaves, seeing:
imprisonment.

Sled:
fun, amusement that doesn't satisfy.

Sleep (cap), hat:
indolence will bring you harm.

Sleep, being disturbed in it:
annoyance.

Sleeping in a car:
experiencing unease and worried times.

Sleeping in a church:
neglecting your business.

Sleeping in a gazebo:
a promising future.

Sleeping with an ugly person:
ill humoured, sickness.

Sleeping with your parents:
happiness, honour, contentment.

Sleepwalker, seeing:
becoming ill.

Sleepwalking:
imminent accident.

Sleeve, taking apart:
divisions.

Sleeves, having wide ones:
acquaintance.

Sleeves, long, seeing:
great honour.

Sleeves, losing:
   return to the beginning, starting over again.

Slippers, worn out:
   annoyance.

Slippers, wearing, walking in:
   good conscience, inner peace.

Sloughy, stepping in or seeing:
   bad luck, annoyance in business deals.

Smallpox, having or seeing:
   receiving money from unexpected circumstances.

Smell, good fragrance:
   loyal friendship.

Smell, bad odour:
   unfaithfulness, phoniness from others.

Smoke, coming through a chimney:
   keeping an engagement, being present.

Smoke, seeing:
   happiness just for show, deception.

Smuggler:
   entanglement, complications.

Snail, seeing:
   good news.

Snake, being bitten by:
   disturbance in a happy relationship.

Snake, killing:
   getting rid of a rival.

Snake, seeing:
   female enemy, being deceived.

Snare (trap), seeing:
   betrayal.

Snipe (bird), eating:
   sadness, acquaintance with false and ungrateful friends.

Snipe (bird), flying:
experiencing lots of changes.

Snow, seeing, walking through:
prospect of multiple luck, flourishing business.

Snow balls, throwing:
injuring your body.

Snowflakes, falling:
receiving good promises.

Soap, using or seeing:
straightening out unclear business, being supported by friends and relatives.

Soap bubbles, blowing:
enjoying brief happiness.

Soap, piece of:
vanity creates damage.

Solar eclipse:
war and hard times.

Soldiers pursuing you:
unrest and bad luck.

Soliciting:
difficulties and misery in the family.

Solicitor, asking you for charity:
cheerfulness.

Solicitor, seeing:
troublesome future.

Solicitor, entering a house:
vexation, annoyance.

Solicitor, sending away:
misery, deficiency, often also prison.

Solicitors, giving something:
success in all ventures; love is being returned without effort.

Soot, finding in your meal:
annoyance.

Soup:
hard consistent work, provides plenty to live on.

Sown, seeing or doing it:
wealth, happiness and health.

Spark, flying around:
a tendency for extravagance.

Sparrow, seeing lots together:
ruin.

Sparrow hawk, catching:
triumph over your enemies.

Spear, seeing:
hate and hostility.

Spectacle (show), seeing or attending:
happiness in marriage, success in deeds.

Spelling, learning:
for those who work, good; for the lazy, bad.

Spider, seeing:
lawsuit.

Spiders:
annoyance, depression, sadness.

Spider, killing:
losing money.

Spider web:
someone is trying to get a secret out of you.

Spine, broken:
losing money, friends, death of a dear relative.

Spine, a long one:
derision, scoffing.

Sponge, to wash yourself, using or seeing:
treason, greed.

Sponge, burning, taking out of your pocket:
escaping danger of fire.

Spoon, seeing:
being invited as a guest.

Sprinter:
precipitance gets you in trouble.

Spruce, seeing or standing under:
being fooled or tricked.

Spurge:
confiding in a disloyal person.

Spur-silver, wearing:
great wealth.

Spy:
beware of inconstancy.

Squirrel, seeing:
for a single woman, good marriage; for a married person, worries about your children.

Squirrel, biting you:
for a single person, bad husband; for a married person, bad children.

Stab, being:
fear and danger.

Stable, being in:
bondage.

Stable, with nice livestock:
prosperity.

Stag (deer), seeing:
gain, profit.

Stairs, seeing:
joy, advantage.

Stairs, walking down:
obtaining treasures.

Stairs, walking up:
  sorrow, sadness.

Stake (post):
  defiance.

Stalk (following):
  dangerous intentions.

Starlings:
  pleasant, joyful news.

Stars, seeing in the sky:
  luck in love, joyful news from friends or relatives.

Stars or shooting stars falling:
  unexpected happiness awaits you.

Statue, seeing:
  embarrassment.

Statue, tipping over, seeing:
  a departure.

Steam engine, seeing:
  great wealth.

Steam ship, traveling on:
  bringing an affair or matter quickly to an end.

Stealing, from you:
  loss of friends.

Stick:
  coming under strict leadership.

Stirrup, seeing:
  going on a trip soon.

Stock (inventory), taking:
  receiving an inheritance.

Stockings, out of silk, putting on:
  poverty.

Stockings, out of cotton or linen:
  changeable luck.

Stockings, pulling down:
  returning happiness.

Stockings, with holes:
  happiness for show, pretending.

Stomach, seeing:
  casualties.

Stone, precious, seeing:
  falling into temptation.

Stone, precious, own:
  great honour.

Stone, precious, receiving:
  increasing wealth.

Stone, precious, wearing:
  arrogance.

Stone chiseling:
  reward for a deserved deed.

Stone, cutting in a quarry:
  obtaining property, real-estate.

Stones, seeing, walking over:
  struggle and suffering.

Stool (human feces), seeing:
  riches, great wealth.

Stool (human feces), stepping into:
  getting an unexpected, large fortune.

Store, with lots of merchandise:
  significant business.

Stork, seeing:
  happy marriage, many children who will turn out well.

Storm, being in it:
  bad luck in love, unfaithfulness.

Storm and rain, experiencing:
  your wishes come true.

Storm, trees falling:
avoiding huge disaster.

Stove, glowing:
becoming lavish, prodigal.

Stove, seeing:
disaster and separation.

Stove pipe, seeing:
small losses.

Strangers, talking to or seeing:
honour and development in your business.

Straw bundle:
prosperity.

Straw mat:
moderation keeps you healthy.

Straw, on fire:
luck and flourishing business.

Straw roof, seeing:
becoming poor through misfortune.

Straw scattered:
misery and annoyance.

Strawberries, eating or seeing:
*joy in your children; late, but good marriage;
success in business; long-lasting health.*

Strawberries, seeing lots:
a growing friendship.

Strawberries, huge, seeing:
means pride.

Strawberries, giving away:
means that you will be well remembered.

Strawberries, picking big ones:
great joy.

Street ballad, singing:
acquaintances bring you into difficult times.

Street, long with nice houses:
being surprised by something beautiful, friendly reception.

Street, with many people:
you will get lots of business.

Stretcher, seeing:
indicates death.

Studying:
long-lasting joy.

Stutter, stammer:
making a strong resolution.

Suburb, seeing:
getting a small profit.

Sugar-sweets, eating:
advantage, profit.

Suitcase, seeing:
forthcoming trip.

Sully and cleaning yourself:
escaping from danger.

Sully, by someone else:
defamation, slander.

Sully, yourself:
unfaithfulness.

Sulphur, seeing:
abolishing false rumours, clearing your name.

Sulphur, striking (as in a match):
imminent and serious illness.

Sulphur, handling:
poor income.

Sun, shining bright:
luck in enterprises, gaining wealth, a position in public office.

Sun, shining in your bed:
serious illness.

Sun, becoming dark:
a bad omen, obstacles in business.

Sun, falling from the sky:
means death of a dignitary.

Sun, reflecting in water:
empty promises.

Sunflower:
honour and prestige.

Sunrise, glowing red:
imminent accident.

Sunset, beautiful seeing:
a peaceful, cheerful life.

Sunset, glowing:
regaining your health.

Swallow, seeing:
a happy message, luck in love.

Swallows, hearing twitter:
settlement in a started dispute.

Swallows nesting in or outside of your house:
steadfast, growing harmony and happiness in your family.

Swallows, flying in swarms:
having a large family.

Swallows, nest:
happy family and rewarding business.

Swamp, stepping into:
misfortune, annoyance in business.

Swans, seeing:
happiness in your marriage, many children; a long and happy life; for a lover, truthful and faithful returning love.

Swearing, or someone else swearing:
unpleasant news, sadness.

Sweeping (a room):
patience in ventures, joyful success.

Sweeping (dirt), and stepping into:
difficulty and trouble in your household.

Sweets, candy, chocolates, eating:
advantage and benefit.

Swellings (tumour), seeing or having:
wealth and riches.

Swimming and sinking:
disaster and prosecution.

Swimming in clear water:
luck and continuous business.

Swimming in cloudy water:
bad omen.

Swimming and having your life in danger:
rescue from danger and trouble.

Swimming and reaching shore:
seeing an almost impossible dream come true.

Swimming and rescuing someone:
escaping a great danger.

Sword, own or having:
experiencing honour.

Sword, nice, polished, receiving:
power, controlling others.

Sword, losing:
losing your established respect.

Sword, breaking apart:
very bad omen.

Sword, with soft handle, getting as a gift:
forthcoming great honour.

Table, seeing decorated:
great joy.

Table, setting yourself:
prosperity and wealth.

Tail, seeing:
being insulted.

Tailor, at his job:
fraud and treason.

Tallow (candle), making or seeing:
achieving rest and peace of mind.

Tar:
be aware of tricky companionship around you.

Task, officially having or receiving:
enduring losses.

Tea, drinking or having:
unclear business.

Tea kettle:
unpleasant messages will surprise you.

Teacher, seeing or talking:
being cheated.

Teeth, losing them:
*losing friends through death or otherwise
unexpected misfortune.*

Teeth, cleaning:
you struggle for others.

Telegraph pole, seeing:
going on a distant trip.

Tenant, seeing:
good social standing, being well-off.

Tent, seeing:
your job is not secure.

Testament:
(see Last Will)

Testimony:
being favoured by a distinguished, noble person.

Theatre:
invitation to parties.

Thermometer:
unstable friendship.

Thieves, breaking in:
good luck and security in business deals.

Thigh, your own, broken:
dying far away from your family, marrying in a foreign country.

Thigh, having nice ones:
luck in trips or undertakings.

Thighs, seeing extremely strong ones:
family and honour.

Thighs, seeing nice ones:
health and happiness.

Thimble, wearing:
hard work and effort are in vain.

Thin (skinny), yourself being:
strong health.

Thirst, cannot be quenched:
endless efforts in some matters, sadness and unrest.

Thirst, to quench excessively:
happiness, honour and great wealth.

Thistles, seeing:
treason, betrayal.

Thorns, being pricked by:
withdrawing from an acquaintance.

Thread, unwinding:
discovery of a secret.

Thread, entangle:
secrets are well protected.

Thread, seeing:
infatuate and charming.

Thresh, seeing:
efforts are in vain.

Throat, seeing:
your hopes are being fulfilled.

Throne:
coming to honour and authority.

Thunder and lightening, hearing or seeing:
being chased into fear.

Thunder and lightening, no damage caused:
happy reunion with a boy- or girlfriend.

Thunder and lightening, catching fire:
experiencing losses before long.

Thunder, without lightening:
a happy message.

Thunder storm:
bad news.

Tie, seeing:
vanity creates heartbreak.

Tied-up, being:
invitation to a rendezvous.

Tin, seeing:
illness.

Tinder:
danger ahead.

Tinker, seeing:
arguments with your neighbours.

Tidbit (little pieces), enjoying:
lack of moderation makes you sick.

Toad, seeing:
losing friends, fraud, pursuit by enemies.

Toad, killing:
triumph over enemies.

Tobacco box:
improving health.

Tobacco, handing out:
annoyance.

Tobacco, taking, inhaling:
forthcoming thirst for pleasure, sex.

Tobacco, pipe, smoking:
success.

Tobacco, pipe, seeing:
arguments.

Tobacco, pipe, breaking apart:
reconciliation with an enemy.

Toilet, lavatory:
annoyance, boredom.

Tongue, seeing:
enduring slander and malignity.

Tools, seeing:
lots of rewarded work ahead.

Toothache:
after sorrow, follows joy.

Toothpick, using or seeing:
very bad omen.

Toothbrush:
a screening in your social circle is necessary.

Torch, carrying:
you are being loved.

Torch, glowing:
shedding light on mysterious, vague matters.

Torch, seeing falling from the sky:
headache.

Torch, putting out:
destroying a comfortable relation.

Torture, suffering from:
lots of distress.

Towel, seeing:
relief from unpleasant people.

Tower, collapsing:
imminent misfortune.

Tower bells, hearing:
you will soon hear pleasant news.

Towers, seeing them in gold:
envy and hate.

Tower, decorated with stone ornaments:
huge advantage.

Toys, seeing:
stay away from childishness.

Trade or trading:
cheating in a business matter.

Trading, bargaining:
business prosperity.

Train, riding in:
matters developing quickly.

Trainstation, seeing:
unexpected visitors.

Trap door:
unexpected good fortune.

Trap, seeing:
wickedness will be clarified.

Travel bag:
a long trip soon takes place.

Treasure of tremendous value, finding:
death or shame.

Treasure, to own or discover:
betrayal by your best friend.

Tree, falling down from:
loss of job, favoritism and prestige.

Tree-garden, seeing:
riches, great wealth.

Tree, harvesting fruits from an old one:
inheritance receiving.

Tree roots, seeing:
becoming ill.

Tree, seeing green and in full bloom:
joy, unexpected enjoyment, happy marriage.

Tree, seeing one which is dry:
indicates death, someone is dying.

Tree, seeing yourself high up in:
power and honour.

Tree, sitting under:
good news is coming.

Tree, split by lightening:
separation of two lovers.

Trees, fallen, destroyed by lightening or burned in half:
annoyance, fear, anxiety, pain, despair.

Trees, on fire:
family quarrels.

Trees, logging:
misfortune.

Trees, picking leaves or fruit:
casualties, losses, illness.

Trees, with lots of fruit, seeing:
profit and wealth.

Trees, without leaves, seeing:
finishing business transactions.

Trip, making:
avoiding vexation.

Trousers:
error, mistake.

Trout (fish), seeing in water:
cheerfulness and love will enhance your life.

Trumpets, hearing:
meeting again, reunion or astonishment.

Trumpet, playing:
hoping for employment.

Turkey (bird), seeing:
being freed from a miserable situation.

Turkish people, seeing:
laziness will hurt you.

Tulips, seeing many beautiful ones:
changing your living standard.

Tulips, having in your room:
coming into better conditions.

Turnpike:
all kinds of obstacles coming your way.

Turtle dove:
unshakable love and friendship.

Turtle, eating:
reaching your goal after putting forth effort for a long time.

Turtle, seeing:
you cherish a secret joy.

U

Udder, of a cow:
blessings, gifts.

Umbrella:
caution when alone, prevention of harm.

Umbrella (sun or rain), seeing or using:
finding support, recommended by sponsors.

Undressing:
bad news.

Uniform, polished, wearing or seeing:
coming to great honour, promotion.

Uplifting, seeing yourself:
great honour.

Urinating:
disagreement.

Urinating and wetting the bed:
clarifying confusing matters.

Urine, drinking:
getting a lot of expenses.

Urn, seeing:
danger ahead.

Vail, wearing:
being respected and loved.

Vampire:
you are slipping into the influence of a swindler.

Vase, with beautiful flowers:
gaining wealth.

Vase, breaking:
losing your boyfriend or girlfriend.

Vat (tub), seeing filled with wine:
good income.

Vat (tub), seeing full but cannot be used:
death in the family.

Vegetables, raw, seeing or eating:
troubled business, annoyance, sickness.

Vehicle, nice one, seeing:
getting to know noble people.

Vehicle, riding in:
prosperity.

Vehicle, sitting in the backseat:
lie, gossip.

Vehicle, seeing turned over:
imminent casualties.

Vehicle, stepping out of it:
loosing your dignitary position.

Vehicle wheel:
embarrassment.

Vein, huge one, seeing:
a scare about your heart.

Velvet:
haughtiness, arrogance brings you down.

Vending-machine, seeing:
profitable business.

Vetch (flower):
your modesty wins new friends.

Villages, seeing:
attending a merry, joyful gathering.

Villages, seeing in prosperity:
indicates happiness.

Villages, poor, visiting:
losing respect, experiencing disdain, contempt.

Villager, seeing or talking to:
happy days ahead.

Vinegar, drinking:
annoyance, dispute in the household, disagreements.

Vinegar, making:
your mind is brewing about evil things.

Vinegar (red), seeing:
abuse.

Vinegar, seeing:
being offended.

Vinegar, spilling:
being accepted with skepticism, disliked.

Vineyard, seeing or walking through:
prosperity, happy family, accommodating friends.

Vintage, gathering:
happiness, honour and riches.

Violets, not yet in bloom:
lawsuit, losing friends and estate.

Violets, seeing in full bloom:
rewarding efforts.

Violets, seeing in summertime:
wealth and honour.

Violin, seeing:
pleasant company.

Violin, holding or playing:
calmness, patience, unpleasant situation.

Viper, seeing:
lucky in love, great wealth.

Visiting someone:
bearing injustice.

Visitors, expecting:
uncomfortable situation ahead.

Vomit, yourself:
for poor people, good omen; for rich people, disadvantage and damage.

Vulture (falcon), seeing:
malicious illness.

Wafer, seeing:
a wished for message, soon to be received.
Waffle:
your thirst for pleasure brings harm.
Walking alone, being lonely:
changeable luck.
Walking and hesitating:
losses and obstacles in business.
Walking, constantly:
careful in your approaches.
Walking fast:
taking on a task without hesitation.
Walking with friends:
stability.
Walking with your lover:
unstable relations.
Wall, collapsing:
misfortune for you or your family.
Wall, in front of you:
annoyance and struggle.
Wall, jumping down from:
joy and fun.
Wall, standing on:
huge success.
Wall, surrounded by water:
coming into disgrace.
Wallpaper, seeing:
joyful news.

Wanderer (traveller):
forthcoming trip.

War cry:
happiness, prayers and wishes are being answered.

War armament:
very bad omen.

War (going to):
conflict with your superior.

Warehouse, being in it:
means betrayal in the open, pursuit.

Wart:
ill-wishing people are getting you in trouble.

Wash basin:
cleanliness is the foundation of health.

Washing, seeing:
libel, slander.

Wasps:
unpleasant complications.

Watch, pocket watch:
good omen.

Water, seeing bright and clear:
prosperity and happiness.

Water, seeing calm and cloudy:
your life is in danger, illness.

Water, warm, drinking:
rejection by friends, sickness.

Water, walking through:
rescue from danger.

Water, having over you:
advantage.

Water, walking on it:
flourishing success.

Water, in a broken glass, cloth or something
that cannot contain it:
bad luck, losses, dishonour.

Water, pure and clear, being offered in a glass:
soon to be married, happy childbirth.

Water pail:
unpleasantness will go away.

Water mill, seeing or being on it:
happiness, wealth, honour

Water snakes:
recovery of the ill and sick.

Water, roaring and sweeping:
bad luck on trips.

Water, being pushed into:
grief and worries.

Water nymph, seeing:
treason, prosecution.

Watering can, seeing:
do not go into extravagances.

Wax, seeing:
be patient and wait, victory is yours.

Weasel, seeing:
malice will harm you.

Weaving, mill:
lots of luck in speculative operations.

Wedding, seeing:
jealousy, lingering illness.

Wedding, having:
damage, losses.

Wedding, marrying another woman when your wife is
still alive:
confusion in your plans.

Wedding, attending and seeing dancing:
means deep sorrow.

Wedding, attending:
joy and good news.

Wedlock:
prosperity, happiness.

Weeds, seeing:
enduring losses.

Weeping:
losing a friend for a long time, sorrow and grief.

Weeping, to see someone:
indicates comfort.

Well, seeing with clear water:
a sincere confession.

Well, strong current:
danger of fire.

Well, bathing in clear water:
escaping from danger.

Well, seeing with beautiful architecture:
receiving nice gifts.

Well, falling into:
in fear of the future.

Well, taking water out:
prosperous business deals.

Whale, seeing:
huge disaster.

Wheat:
hard work brings prosperity.

Wheat field in bloom:
wealth and honourable love, all wishes coming true in marriage, many well-mannered children.

Wheel or wheelwork, seeing:
forthcoming illness.

Wheels, seeing turning:
quickly reaching the goal you hoped for.

Wheel of fortune, seeing:
misfortune or annoyance.

Wheelbarrow, being pulled by dogs:
despair.

Whet (stone), seeing:
good results in trade or trading.

Whey, drinking:
worrying about your health.

Whip, seeing:
beware of punishment.

Whip, swinging:
making friends through honesty.

Whistle, trying to but can't:
obstacles in your plans.

Whistle, hearing:
being warned about something.

Whiskers, having on yourself:
idle, transient joy.

White grouse, flying:
unexpected news.

Whore, seeing or talking to:
happy days ahead, luck.

Whorehouse, seeing:
misfortune, pursuit, illness.

Widow, being:
receiving satisfaction.

Wife, talking to:
unstable changes in business.

Wig:
vanity brings you sorrow.

Will-o-the-wisp:
seduction and dishonesty are harmful.

Wind, feeling:
good event, joyful news.

Window, at the rear side of a building, on fire:
losing close relatives.

Window, at the front, on fire:
death of a relative or acquaintance.

Window, climbing out:
bad luck in business.

Window, seeing open:
happiness in your household.

Window, seeing closed:
means things are coming down hard on you

Window, you falling out:
means lawsuits.

Window, stepping through:
being accepted in a positive and friendly way.

Windowpane, seeing:
complicated situation.

Wine, spilling:
losing respect.

Wine, seeing:
hemorrhage warning.

Wine, drinking a good one:
showing resistance

Wine, mixed with water, drinking:
illness or changing luck in business.

Wine soup, eating:
indisposition.

Wine and getting drunk:
receiving love and respect from a noble superior, happiness in the future.

Wings, having and flying:
good for everybody.

Wire, plain, seeing:
traps being set.

Wire, made out of copper:
profitable, lucky, ongoing business.

Witch, seeing:
being involved with a greedy person.

Wives, seeing many:
change and variation.

Wolf, biting you:
slander, libel.

Wolf, killing:
getting rid of a bad, tricky enemy.

Woman, (whore) being in the company of:
gossip, inconstancy.

Woman, being favoured by them:
arguments ahead.

Woman, clothes, wearing:
sorrow, misfortune.

Woman, courting:
being cheated by flatterers.

Woman, fooling around with:
dispute about inheritance.

Woman, having more than one:
being tormented.

Woman, old with white hair:
losses of many kinds.

Woman, seeing beautiful and being in love:
happiness, health and wealth.

Woman, seeing pregnant:
good news.

Nostradamus' Egyptian Dream Interpretation Book

Woman, seeing with beautiful, long hair:
   honour and wealth, happy union.

Woman, seeing with black hair:
   uneasiness and sorrow.

Woman, seeing with brown hair:
   illness.

Woman, seeing with red hair:
   being pursued.

Woman, unknown, seeing or talking to:
   acquaintance.

Wood, cutting:
   diligence and progress.

Wood, carrying:
   becoming poor.

Wood, logging:
   a death.

Wood, picking up or seeing piled up:
   grief, a lot of affliction.

Woodframing:
   great honour.

Wood, throwing into the fire:
   waste, extravagance.

Wood, floating on water:
   devastation in your longing for happiness.

Wooden shoes, seeing or wearing:
   modest, but happy family life.

Wooden vessel, seeing:
   economical—modesty keeps you away from starvation

Wool, buying or selling:
   luck in business, making good money, respected by authority.

World ending:
   stupidity creates obstacles.

Working:
: *a good continuation in ventures.*

Worms, seeing:
: *careful—evil is around you.*

Worms, killing:
: *being set free from drawbacks.*

Wound (sore), seeing or being wounded yourself:
: *good prospect in projects, harmony in the family, false friends are giving up on you.*

Wounded person, seeing:
: *your lack of consideration means disadvantage to others.*

Wreath, carrying:
: *means, mark of salute.*

Wreath made of myrtle, seeing:
: *a wedding.*

Wreath, making:
: *diligence.*

Wreath, seeing at a funeral or by graves:
: *inheritance, or losing your loved ones.*

Wreath, woven from evergreens:
: *fulfillment of your hopes.*

Wrestle:
: *quarrel and dispute.*

Wrestle with a beast:
: *defamation.*

Wrestle with a stranger:
: *imminent danger.*

Wrinkles in your face, seeing:
: *reaching an old age.*

Writer, in an office or public office:
: *coming into a confusing situation.*

Wrought-iron, making:
: *dispute, argument.*

Wrought-iron, seeing or being hit:
great losses.

Wrought-iron, seeing red hot:
intimate love, high blood pressure, nervousness.

Yard, seeing messy:
   disparage.

Yard, spanning a net over it:
   great wealth.

Yard or farm, your own:
   rich inheritance.

Yarn, entangled:
   lovers chasing each other.

Yarn, to unwind:
   prone to lavishness, to discover a secret.

Yarn, to wind up:
   becoming greedy.

Yasmine (gazebo):
   forthcoming engagement.

Yeast, eating:
   prolonging physical suffering.

Young, becoming:
   vanity causes heartbreak.

Youth, seeing a young man:
   only your own strength leads to prosperity.

Nostradamus' Egyptian Dream Interpretation Book

Zebra, seeing:
don't befriend fools.

Zero (number), seeing:
riches, wealth, honour, good fortune in ventures.

Zither, playing:
appearing pleasant in society.

MEANING OF DREAMS—
ACCORDING TO THE
ZODIAC

There are many dreams that are independent of time and place and have their own meaning altogether. And yet, the same dream could have different meanings, depending on which Zodiac sign the Earth was in when the dream occurred.

To determine more information about a dream in relation to the Zodiac, you must first remember the images you saw in the dream. Then, you have to determine (using an astrological calendar) which sign the Earth was moving at the time that you had the dream. Once you've done this, you can use the following chart to discover the meaning behind the dream.

For example:

If you dream about a visit from a good friend when the Earth is in Leo, look at the chart under number 9 and then move over to Leo. Your dream means 'Honour'.

If you dream about music and instruments when the Earth is in Capricorn, look at the chart under number 14, and then move over to Capricorn. Your dream means 'Comfort', which explains again, what lies ahead.

Nostradamus' Egyptian Dream Interpretation Book

Kind of Dream Dreaming of:	I Aries	2 Taurus	3 Gemini	4 Cancer	5 Leo
1. Money and all kinds of Coins	Illness	Punishment	Loss of a friend	Visitor	Money
2. Fish and aquatic animals	Anxiety	Comfort	Honour	Mental-suffering	Anxiety or harm
3. Kisses, caresses	Unpleasantness	Trip	Visitor	A friend	Advantage, and profit
4. Large Gathering	News	Violent dispute	Emotion	Joy	Gift
5. Illness, physical discomfort	Joyful surprise	Joy	Cheat	Losses	Noble friends
6. Meals, and edible Foods	Joy	Visitors	Joy	Annoyance	Long-lasting life
7. Misfortunes of all kinds	Request in vain	Lies	Respectful to others	Weakness	Affliction, grief
8. Churches, Houses, Towers, Buildings in general	Joy	Anguish of mind	Serious illness	Money	Soon to get visitors
9. Arrival or visiting of good Friends	Gift	Secret enjoyment	Pleasantness	Gain, profit	Honour
10. Fire, Thunder, and shooting	Sadness	Guests	Profit	Drunkenness	Losses
11. Fire, (any type of)	Sadness	Misery and grief	Weakness	Affliction	Rule, mastery, control
12. Body weakness, painful joints	Good things	Sadness	Sorrow	Hopes in vain	New friendship alliance

Nostradamus' Egyptian Dream Interpretation Book

6 Virgo	7 Libra	8 Scorpio	9 Sagittarius	10 Capricorn	11 Aquarius	12 Pisces
Cheerful-ness	Death of a relative	Theft	Joy	Joy	Losses	Effort
Death of a friend	Health	Pleasant surprise	Sorrow	Hostility	Illness	Illness
Kindness, good	Invitation	News	Fraud	Loneliness	Odd joy	Changing opinion
Happiness	Misfortune	Joy	Enjoyment	Loss of a friend	Love-affair	Lots of joy
Merriness	Comfort	Dispute	Unhappy love	A friend	Effort	Worries
Illness	Appre-hension	Fear anxiety	Comfort	Profit	Severe arguments	Joy
Trouble deficiency	Illness of a friend	Losses	Winning over a new friend	Pain	Pleasant-ness	Anxious
Lots of Luck	Advantage	Joy	A Friend	Affliction grief	Restlessness	Good news
Fear, fright	Sadness, grief	Wealth	Honour	Important event	Sadness	Anger
Sadness	Joy	Weakness	Illness	Visitor	Pain	Great fear
Gain, profit	Surprise	Death	Death	Dispute	Marriage	Joy
Joy	Worry, grief	Illness	Cheerfulness	Need, distress	Money	Expenses

Nostradamus' Egyptian Dream Interpretation Book

Kind of Dream Dreaming of:	1 Aries	2 Taurus	3 Gemini	4 Cancer	5 Leo
13. Work-equipment, Tools or instruments	Dispute, money	Profit	Good things	Gain through a death case	Very pleasant visitors
14. Singing, music, playing of instruments	Very bad news	Travel	Unexpected joy	Sadness	Deception
15. Tears, and deep sorrow	Arguments about religion	Vain worries, fear	Joy	Illness	Profit
16. Arguments, dispute, fights, war	Weakness	Victory over your enemy	Pleasantness	Honour	Envy
17. Dead bodies, funeral	Marriage	Winning in the lottery	Misfortune	Dispute	Profit
18. Urinating	Losses	Sadness	Idle hopes	Annoyance	Delight
19. Exile, expulsion, abuse	Fraud	Joy	Good things	Guests	Gift
20. Giants, ghosts, monsters	Anxiety	Dispute	Moral aberration	Well being	Illness
21. Horses, huge animals, riders, drivers	Weakness	Honour	Loosing a friend	Surprise	Long life
22. Murder, killing, bloodshed	Grief, deep sorrow	Loss of a friend	Intimacy, familiarity	Richness, wealth	Illness
23. Joy, Cheerfulness, entertainment	Sorrow, affliction	Foolishness	Money	Cheerfulness	Envy
24. New, fine cloth, linen sheets	Intoxication	Joy	Annoyance	Guests or dinner party	Hostility

Nostradamus' Egyptian Dream Interpretation Book

6 Virgo	7 Libra	8 Scorpio	9 Sagittarius	10 Capricorn	11 Aquarius	12 Pisces
A girlfriend	Theft	Honour	Unpleasant news	Worries	Comfort	News
Strange events	Fooled hopes	Grieve through a friend	Acquaintance	Comfort	Pleasant things	Arguments
Joy	Pleasing surprise	Amusement, fun	Fright, fear	Death of a relative	Death of a superior	Enemies
Pleasing things	Pleasant news	Good money making	Pleasing news	Dispute	Being merry	Tears
Disagreement	Grief, worries	Joy	Shock, terror	Surprise	Enormous luck	Lottery –win
Illness	Joy	Fright	War	Unexpected friends	Love	Happiness
Grief	Bad things	Death of a relative	Move, moving	Guests	Hostility	Joy
Money	Joyful, happy	Death of a friend	Enormous luck	Joy	Joy	Visitor
Argument	Degrading	Sadness	Fraud	Liable, slander	Dinner with guests	Deception
Pain	Concern, trouble	Harm	Early death	Losses	Fraud	Advantage
Pleasantness	Unpleasantness	Affliction, distress	Joy	Delightfulness	Profit	Joy
Dispute	Joy	Honour	Losses	News	Injury, harm	Hostility

Chart of Luck and Unlucky Days

LUCKY DAYS

January	1	3	10	27	31
February	7	8	18		
March	5	9	12	14	16
April	5	17			
May	1	2	4	9	14
June	3	5	7	12	25
July	2	6	10	23	30
August	4	7	10	14	20
September	6	10	13	17	30
October	15	16	25	31	
November	1	15	25	30	
December	10	20	29		

UNLUCKY DAYS

January	13	23		
February	2	10	17	22
March	13	19	23	28
April	18	20	29	30
May	10	17	20	
June	4	20		
August	5	13	27	31
September	13	16	18	26
October	3	9	27	
November	6	23		
December	15	26	31	

Birth Month—Characteristics

January   **A male** born in January has many talents but little pride. With much effort he will become a real go-getter. He enjoys being around positive people and has much luck and happiness in marriage. He has the potential to strike it rich.

A female born in January can never have enough lovers, despite her cold-hearted feelings. She will marry a well-off man, but will cause trouble for her husband.

February   **A male** born in February has a strong spiritual drive, as well the ability to handle both physical and spiritual pressure. He loves gambling, riding horses and driving cars. He is careless and foolish, but in the end, he will find happiness.

A female born in February is not very well-read. She pretends to love books, but secretly wishes nothing more than to be married.

March   **A male** born in March has an unstable nature, and therefore has difficulty making decisions. Despite his insecurity, he does not stay single. His earnings and achievements will provide a comfortable lifestyle for him in his old age.

A female born in March loves men very much, but is clever enough to hide her weakness. She is known to visit fortune tellers, and is shocked by things she doesn't want to hear.

April   A male born in April is honourable, witty and pleasure-seeking. His trickster-like character suits him well. He enjoys success in education and employment, but shows little interest in marriage.

A female born in April has a surly, sullen nature. She desires marriage at a young age and has many expectations about her relationship. After her wedding, she will often sing this song:

Those who expect from the golden ring only golden days, Oh they don't know the course of life, and not the hearts of men.

May   A male born in May is diligent and skillful, but has a very stubborn character. In his married life he will have a lot of obstacles to overcome.

A female born in May is witty and jolly, but also very conscientious. She wins over many friends, but finds it difficult to acquire wealth.

June   A male born in June shows little interest in education or work. However, he manages to get by with what he inherits from his mother.

A female born in June is very lady-like and able to mask her feelings. She combines female affection with man-like steadfastness. She is good-hearted, but fights back if someone tries to do wrong. She loves money, but manages to live in a modest fashion.

July   **A male** born in July has many talents but will develop only a few. He has a tendency to boast about his heroism, although much of this is fabricated. He is always speculating and would love nothing more than to find a rich bride.

A female born in July is hungry for knowledge and she studies a lot. Although she does not like to cook, she will be a good housewife. Her husband will have nothing to complain about except her superior intellect.

August   **A male** born in August has a very jealous nature, but he manages to hide it most of the time. He doesn't have much luck with women. He will live a long life.

A female born in August has a compassionate nature and, therefore, is vulnerable to objectionable happenings. She does not want to remain single.

September **A male** born in September has a large ego and is quick to quarrel with others. He does not listen to warnings and has many enemies. However, in marriage he is a loving, caring husband.

A female born in September is always worrying, even when there is nothing to worry about. She is a pet-lover throughout her life, makes her husband very happy and is a good money-manager.

October   **A male** born in October is cheerful and merry. He is attracted to females from an early age and is drawn to them his whole life. In marriage he can be extremely happy.

A female born in October tends, even at an early age, to play the 'wise guy'. She is more drawn to a high-ranked man than any other one. She is not opposed to marrying a widower without children.

November   **A male** born in November is very carefree. He likes to play the role of master, and does not hesitate to fabricate stories. In marriage, he has a chance to eliminate some of his mistakes.

A female born in November is naughty and witty, pays a lot of attention to her appearance and never says "no" when being asked for a dance. She prefers the company of men to women, and will marry at a young age.

December **A male** born in December is successful in ventures that do not involve a lot of thought. He likes to reach for higher goals, but will always be satisfied with the woman he has chosen.

A female born in December has a tendency to flirt. Even though she receives a great deal of flattery, she shows tremendous steadfastness.

Fingernail Characteristics

BY COLOUR

Pale and lead-coloured nails...

indicate a melancholic person who prefers a quiet lifestyle that includes studying and spiritual activity.

White nails...

indicate a person of thin, dainty stature who enjoys being in love, but who has stomach problems.

White nails with lead-coloured spots...

indicate a person who leans toward a melancholic nature but is easily irritated.

BY SHAPE

Wide nails...

indicate a soft, emotional, warm-hearted person who is also very shy.

Wide nails surrounded by damaged skin...

indicate a person who indulges in risk-free delights and amusements.

Wide nails with white spots...

indicate a very careless person who will let luck run right through his/her hands.

Fleshy, thick nails...

> indicate a calm, composed person who loves to sleep, eat and drink, and who finds enjoyment in the activities of others.

Long nails...

> indicate a well-mannered, good natured person who, according to others, has achieved inner peace, but will never become rich.

Round nails...

> indicate someone with an angry but goodhearted character who is fond of science. He or she is somewhat willful and self-conceited about the beauty of their body.

Small nails...

> characterize a very nosy person who has the misfortune of having a loose tongue.

Rough nails...

> indicate a person with a jolly nature. This person loves to be alive and wishes it will never end.

Ace

King

Major/
Queen

Ten

Jack

The German Deck

The Art of Laying the Cards with the German Deck

*T*he following chapter will introduce you to the art of conducting your own 'reading'. The famous French fortune-teller *le Normand's* technique is explained.

Throughout her long successful career, she was convinced, that readings she achieved with the German-Deck, were more accurate readings, than with the French-Tarot. Even in her most difficult cases she used the German set of cards, consisting of 32 pieces. She shuffled them well. Her client had to lift them with the left hand in two portions, placing each of them next to the main pile. Remember the sequence, because the third and last section, you pick up and place it on the first and main pile. Together drop them onto the middle or second section. Don't shuffle them again, but instead lay them in 4 rows, with each 8 cards on display.

The meaning of the single cards in four different colors are explained!

Heart (red)

Red is recognized by this set of cards as the principal color. Heart-King represents a male person for whom the reading is done. Heart-Queen—always indicates the female person, for whom the cards are being read. Those two figures King and Queen are the principals in all other colors. The color "red" represents in general love and happiness.

The meaning of the following single cards are:

1) *heart Ace*:   laying next to the principal (King or Queen) means the home of that person, or it can belong to someone else. Overall it means a large building or a house.

2) *heart King*:   is the male for whom you are reading the cards. If you have a female client, the King is pointing to a man whom she is acquainted with, or is in some relationship. It can also mean a lover or a close relative.

3) *heart Queen*:   indicates the lady for whom the cards are read. It can also be a young lady, a sweetheart, a sister, or a close female relative.

4) *heart Jack*:   shows the thoughts of the person, for whom reading is done. The thoughts correspond to the other cards surrounding the Heart-Jack.

5) *heart Ten*:   the card of Marriage status. It means for a single person a marriage in the near future. Whereas for a married person it means occurrences or events in relation to the other cards around it.

6) *heart Nine*:   tender, loving affections.

7) *heart Eight*:	a certainty and assurance in a particular matter.
8) *heart Seven*:	means only one living room, (comparing to the living quarters in a whole house, as in 1) Ace).

Leaf (green)

This color is neutral, and has no definite meaning, but in general it points to good, lovely influences.

1) *green Ace*:	a public-office or courthouse.
2) *green King*:	a young man.
3) *green Queen*:	a young girl, in case if more of these cards a scattered it points to "single" persons, but if they lay next to each other, it points to a married couple. If two cards of "Jack" are laying above each other in two different rows, this indicates Mother and Son. If two cards of "Jack" are laying under each other in the 3th and 4th row, it means Father and Daughter. The same meaning belongs to all other colors of that particular card.
4) *green Jack*:	a messenger, or thoughts.
5) *green Ten*:	a pleasant letter.

6) *green Nine*: a trip, or travelling far distance.

7) *green Eight*: enjoying a stroll, or walking short distances.

8) *green Seven*: is a warning, beware of everything around you. If this card is near a female, that means a cradle (Baby) or a marriage, but without the blessing of the church. For a male, it also could mean a baby without wedlock, which creates an unpleasant situation.

Schelle (bell)

This color of cards means Money, if more of the same Schelle are laying together, means more money. In general, this card indicates mostly Profit through Speculation, Inheritance or Lottery.

1) *schelle Ace*: enormous happiness.

2) *schelle King*: a rich young man.

3) *schelle Queen*: a wealthy girl.

4) *schelle Jack*: a gift, or something else good.

5) *schelle Ten*: a letter with money.

6) *schelle Nine*: money in general.

7) *schelle Eight*: lesser money.

8) *schelle Seven*: even less money.

Acorn (yellow)

Which ever way these cards lay, it indicates 'bad' influences. If any card of this color lies near the principal, it means illness. Should some cards of Jack lay under the principal, that could mean death.

The meaning of the rest of these cards are as follows:

1) *acorn Ace:*   scare, shock, but if there is a Heart or Schelle-card close to the Ace, it means a joyful shock.

2) *acorn King:*   pointing to an older Gentleman, or man.

3) *acorn Queen:*   a female person beware of, unless there are good cards surrounding her.

4) *acorn Jack:*   many confusing, tainted thoughts

5) *acorn Ten:*   an unpleasant letter.

6) *acorn Nine:*   anger and annoyance.

7) *acorn Eight:*   grief, repulsiveness.

8) *acorn Seven:*   tears.

The last edition of Nostradamus' Egyptian Dream Interpretation Book, 1928, also contained material on other kinds of magic and mysticism, no doubt in view of the curiosity many people have about the invisible influences on the world from beyond. The most popular method of doing so, which has survived to the present day, is the art of laying out cards. Many continue to seek answers and advice for the future in this way.

My intention in including it in this new edition is that it should be thought of as an entertainment to be indulged in, typically, in private and in the home.

Which is alright, as long as we keep in mind 'that it is only our own volition, setting in motion the law of cause and effect, that we should use to master our destiny.'

So, have fun.

Dreams

Represented in

Pictures

Nostradamus' Egyptian Dream Interpretation Book

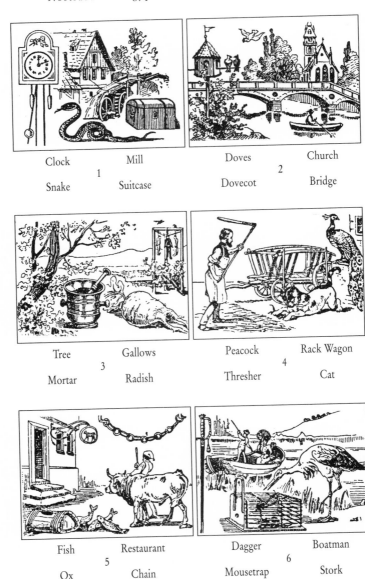

Clock   Mill
            1
Snake   Suitcase

Doves   Church
            2
Dovecot   Bridge

Tree   Gallows
            3
Mortar   Radish

Peacock   Rack Wagon
            4
Thresher   Cat

Fish   Restaurant
            5
Ox   Chain

Dagger   Boatman
            6
Mousetrap   Stork

Nostradamus' Egyptian Dream Interpretation Book

Bags of Money	Graveyard	Shooting	Mirror
7		8	
Frogs	Funeral	Flea	Knife and Fork

Thunder	Bear	Mountain	Flies
9		10	
Hat	Oven	Pot	Night Watchman

Fire	Bushes	Plough	Lighter
11		12	
Basket	Camel	Turk	Flat Iron

Fortress	Mushrooms		Barrel	Pub, Beer House
	13			14
Goat	Sentry		Books	Dog

Stable	Dry Tree		Garden	Hermit
	15			16
Sickle	Whip		Death's Skull	Cave

Coffin	Lemon		Smoke Pan	Stars
	17			18
Wanderer	Dress Material		Vomiting	Child-Bed Illness

Nostradamus' Egyptian Dream Interpretation Book

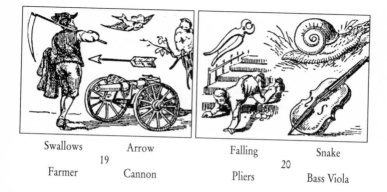

Swallows	Arrow	Falling	Snake
19		20	
Farmer	Cannon	Pliers	Bass Viola

Lavatory	Fighting	Dancing	Fruit
21		22	
Sheep	Roost Ladder	Violin	Sausages

Mountain-House	Chandelier	Cheese	Thief
23		24	
Torte-Pastry	Dead Body	Eggs	Rabbit

Barracks	Horseman
	25
Toys	Wooden Barrel

Jack-Daw	Carpet
	26
Studying	Tooth

Bell	Pitcher
	27
Torch	Driving

Bread	Ladder
	28
Newspaper	Frying Pan

Jacket	Rat
	29
Sleeping	Silver Coins

Wind	Scale
	30
Cross	Haywagon

Nostradamus' Egyptian Dream Interpretation Book

Overcoat	Nails
	31
Hatchet	Bricklayer

Boots	Coal
	32
Grapes	Nurse

Drinking	Tobacco-Pipe
	33
Eyeglasses	Purse

Baking Oven	Flag
	34
Frighten	Despair

Stockings	Girl
	35
Beggar	Tower

Chimney	Pencil
	36
Drum	Beheading-Execution

Mask	Ox
37	
Eggshells	Trout

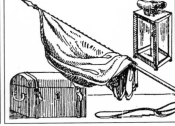

Banner	Lantern
38	
Chest-Suitcase	Spoon

Stairs	Raven
39	
Old-Women	Anchor

Rooster	Flowers
40	
Letter	Swimming

Plums	Fruit-Tree
41	
Roof	Man with Nightcap

Sugar Piece	Crab
42	
Bowling	Snuffbox

Nostradamus' Egyptian Dream Interpretation Book

Ghost	Basket
	43
Bread	Waterpail

Bee's	Pursuit
	44
Wolf	Shoe

Black-Person	Deer
	45
Bellows	Butcher

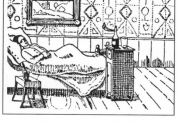

Picture	Wallpaper
	46
Sickness	Medicine

Spider	Hop
	47
Invalid	Hen

Confessional	Harp
	48
Child	Prison

Nostradamus' Egyptian Dream Interpretation Book

Jew	Village
	49
Turtle	Wheel

Kissing	Slipper
	50
Lock	Luggage Carrier

Praying Nun	Cellar
	51
Whetstone	Bonnet

Servant	Cards
	52
Dice	Coffee Drinker

Lard pot	Duck
	53
Sedan-Chair	Combing

Roast	Cabbage
	54
Lettuce	Gnome

Nostradamus' Egyptian Dream Interpretation Book

Stick		Horseshoe
	55	
Wheat		Cow

Corsetry		Key
	56	
Candles		Money Counting

Leafless Tree		Birds
	57	
Pocket Watch		Fencer

Flowers		Cooking
	58	
Fish		Bun

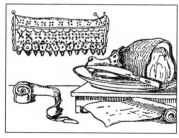

Lace		Ham
	59	
Ribbon		Canvas

Sewing		Skating
	60	
Knitting		Bench

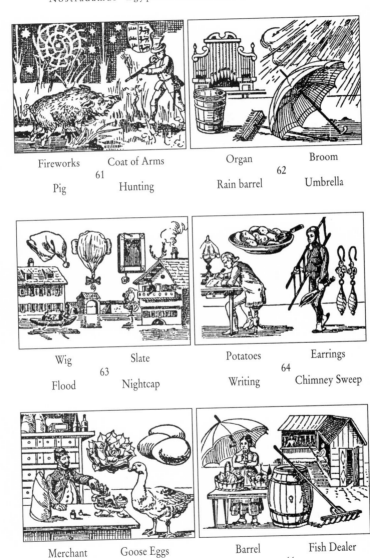

Fireworks	Coat of Arms	Organ	Broom
	61		62
Pig	Hunting	Rain barrel	Umbrella
Wig	Slate	Potatoes	Earrings
	63		64
Flood	Nightcap	Writing	Chimney Sweep
Merchant	Goose Eggs	Barrel	Fish Dealer
	65		66
Vegetable	Goose	Trading Post	Rake

Nostradamus' Egyptian Dream Interpretation Book

Blind Man   Lion

67

Dog   Leather

Altar   Procession

68

Lamp   Preacher

Hall   Slipper

69

Soldiers-Prisoner   Pump

Nun   Scissor

70

Pail   Beggar

Shirt   Collar-Neckband

71

Cloth   Bed

Jewels   Arm Chair

72

Table   Curtain

Nostradamus' Egyptian Dream Interpretation Book

Lily	Glove	Sun	Moon
73		74	
Monk	Sled	Pole Sticks	Earthquake
Actor/Theatre	Reading	Saw	Coffee Mug
75		76	
Fig	Dinner/Table	Bowl	Tent
Humming Iron	Wild Geese	Doctor	Cage
77		78	
Carpenter's Bench	Drunken Man	Chapel	Iron

Nostradamus' Egyptian Dream Interpretation Book

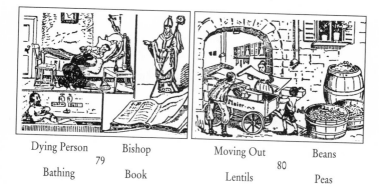

Dying Person	Bishop		Moving Out	Beans
	79			80
Bathing	Book		Lentils	Peas

Comb	Old Man		Vineyard	Accident
	81			82
Bowl	Woman		Tie	Vegetable Garden

Darkness	Billiard Table		Playing Cards	Sleep Walker
	83			84
Watering Can	Rainbow		Coffee Mill	Stones

Nostradamus' Egyptian Dream Interpretation Book

Wood Pile	Sieve
85	
Box	Nobleman

Barrel	Wheels
86	
Grasshopper	King's Carriage

School	Buckle
87	
Trumpet	Kettle Drum

Vicious Dog	Broom
88	
Fan	Spin

Fool	Pistol
89	
Glass	Kettle

Monkey	Giant
90	
Greenhouse	Muff

Nostradamus' Egyptian Dream Interpretation Book

The End

———————————

German Edition 1928

NOSTRADAMUS—
EPILOGUE

*M*ichel Nostradamus' fame has lasted for over 500 years, and it will outlive many generations yet to come. I feel I owe homage to this wise man, but not only because of his mastery of the subjects he studied. I pay tribute to him, because not only was the knowledge he manifested based on the foundations already given by the Creator in the form of the Universal Governing Laws; rather, by obeying those Laws, he went further and achieved new knowledge.

All of the high civilizations of history left traces of themselves that have survived to the present day in what we call 'myths'. While their details may have become blurred with the passage of time, at their core remain indications of an understanding of Universal Divine Law. This quality ensures their survival, because their very nature is beyond the limitations of space and time, and partakes of eternity.

These facts, these Universal Laws, can never change. As long as human beings fail to apply them, which hold heaven, earth and ourselves together in balanced harmony, and consider them a matter of priority as the foundation for our very lives, we will never succeed in making the world a better and more peaceful place. If each individual conducted his or her personal affairs with them in mind, we would, by making that conscious choice, all thereby contribute—directly or indirectly—toward leaving real, worthy, and permanent values for ourself and our descendants. What lasting benefit can come from following any cause or pursuing any purpose, however good it might seem, when that cause is formulated with respect to only one of those vitally important Universal Laws, and not all of them?

The time has passed, when only a privileged few can have Knowledge of those Laws and apply their understanding of them. It is available here, now, for all who seek greater insight into the interconnection of all activity in Creation; it is explained, with no omissions, in the book entitled *In the Light of Truth*.

Let me summarize in simple words.

Only if we try to understand the interwoven rules and regulations the Creator has implemented for us, his temporary guests on earth, will we be able to achieve right behavior in the sense of conducting our lives according to His Will. The divine Master laid down the railway tracks at the beginning. The destination of the rolling train is predetermined for every traveller. We are free to choose in which wagon we want to ride. Through exercising our Free Will, we can if we wish, decide to jump off or onto the journey, provided that we never lose sight of the train in motion, decorated with the menu of guidelines on display for all who have it in mind to reach their destination according to "Master's Blueprint".

Do we not all hope for the best journey possible until the last station is reached? How can we be sure of our arrival, if we deliberately deny, through wilful ignorance, His Knowledge of how to get there? Only by making the effort to understand His 'travel guide' in order to stay on track, do we have the chance to avoid missing the connecting train that awaits each traveller at the earthly end-station. The transition of 'changing trains' may be bumpy or smooth, depending on what we have earned through our life experiences so far. Either way, the next train will see our journey continuing through a realm with a different landscape. The way to make sure of that is to follow our own perception from the "travel guide" where our journey is explained in fine detail and clarity, in the

"Living Book of Life"…

IN THE LIGHT OF TRUTH
The Grail Message

by ABD-RU-SHIN

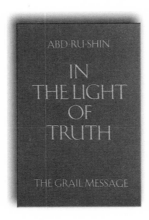

This classic work occupies a unique place among all books written. The Grail Message of Abd-ru-shin mediates the Knowledge of the upbuilding of Creation.

In simple words, it explains the connections without a gap, and gives a complete survey of all the activity in Creation. This work, of only 168 lectures deals with all essential questions and spheres of life: natural science, ethnology, social and economic questions, religion and church, psychology and cultivation of the spirit, family and state, sex and sexuality, occultism, justice and law, knowledge and wisdom, the world, time and eternity, the recognition of God, and many other topics.

Available in 15 languages in 52 countries.

Original edition: German
Also available in: English, French, Dutch, Italian, Spanish, Portuguese, Rumanian, Hungarian, Slovak, Czech, Russian, Finnish, Swedish and Arabic.
In preparation: Chinese

On sale in bookstores and from Grail Publications:

Canada: Grail Publications, P.O. Box 412, Chénéville, PQ   JOV 1E0
Tel/fax: (819) 428-2898 or 1-800-672-2898
U.S.A.: Grail Foundation Press, P.O.Box 45, Gambier OH 43022
Tel: 1-800-427-9217; Fax: 1-614-427-4954

www.grailmessage.com

BÖHMEN

About the Author

Dietlinde (Dita) Arzt was born in Sudetenland (Bohemia).

In 1945 Dita, then a small child, experienced with her family the atrocities of war, despite the official declaration of "the second world war is over". With her family she was expelled from her beloved homeland and the estate, that had been theirs for 700 years. Her family can be traced as far back as the year 1228 to her German ancestry, where she was able to return to her roots of origin in 1946-47.

Dita has always been, and remains today, intensely grateful to her parents for having not only provided a loving and caring home for her and her two sisters even as Germany lay in ruins, but for demonstrating excellence of character and profound inner strength and thereby planting in her the seeds, so vital for any young life, of the stability essential for all future personal growth.

In 1952 Dita, then employed as an intern in a trading company, was introduced to *Nostradamus' Egyptian Dream Interpretation Book* by one of her working colleagues. She was astonished to find that its predictions came true, as they continue to come true today; but the joy she experienced in the sense of having found, as it were, a secret companion, one who could help her glimpse the future, was tempered by the discovery that the volume was no longer in print. Her fascination with the great seer and astrologer was nevertheless established, and endured for decades to come.

Dita made the decision to leave her home in 1960 to 'explore the world on her own' and moved to Munich, where great opportunities opened as she pursued the career of her dreams as a model and actor. She succeeded, but preferred to continue in her business career. Progress in her profession required her to travel internationally, and her destiny brought her to Canada in 1969, where she married and started a family. In addition to raising her two daughters, Dita and Cora, Dita once again, climbed the ladder of the corporate word. For twenty-five years she occupied the position of vice-president of a successful international company. But, not enough, at the age of fifty, she again, successfully, tested her gifts as an actress and model in Toronto.

Recently retired from public life, Dita now dedicates her time to her long-standing literary interests, to delve into and expose life's secrets. She is compelled to devote her first writing to sharing with the world, the last remaining copy of Nostradamus' volume on dream interpretations, on the occasion of its 500th anniversary.